Elephants Never Lie

One Woman's Inner Journey to Release the Emotional Weight

MICHELLE LUCAS

BALBOA.
PRESS
A DIVISION OF HAY HOUSE

Balboa Press books may be ordered through booksellers or by contacting:

Balboa Press
A Division of Hay House
1663 Liberty Drive
Bloomington, IN 47403
www.balboapress.com
1 (877) 407-4847

Because of the dynamic nature of the Internet, any web addresses or
links contained in this book may have changed since publication and
may no longer be valid. The views expressed in this work are solely those
of the author and do not necessarily reflect the views of the publisher,
and the publisher hereby disclaims any responsibility for them.

The author of this book does not dispense medical advice or prescribe the use
of any technique as a form of treatment for physical, emotional, or medical
problems without the advice of a physician, either directly or indirectly. The
intent of the author is only to offer information of a general nature to help
you in your quest for emotional and spiritual well-being. In the event you use
any of the information in this book for yourself, which is your constitutional
right, the author and the publisher assume no responsibility for your actions.

Any people depicted in stock imagery provided by Getty Images are
models, and such images are being used for illustrative purposes only.
Certain stock imagery © Getty Images.

Print information available on the last page.

ISBN: 978-1-9822-3373-0 (sc)
ISBN: 978-1-9822-3374-7 (e)

Library of Congress Control Number: 2019912543

Balboa Press rev. date: 09/09/2019

Foreword

Like a rose gives its life to the sun, Rebecca gives her heart. She is generous, kind and loving. Rebecca wants others to feel good, so she gives her love in spades. One moment her heart is open, touching every soul that comes into reach. The lost, the suffering, the lonely. Her lover. Then the pain hits. With betrayal her heart withers in the overwhelming understanding that her reality is nothing like her heart. Fear sets in and she can no longer blossom into a world too eager to pick her away.

You see, Rebecca lives with love, but she sleeps with demons. Of course she does not know this yet, but she does call them by name. Longing. Despair. Anguish. Fear. Holding them, she creates suffering, a suffering that bursts like the sun stinging the skin into a burning anxiety. She believes that ripping love from her life is either God's cruel test of her faith or her own lack of patience. She has yet to discover that her extreme sensitivities, feeling the feelings of others, is her strength, a strength that is enmeshed in a web of her greatest gifts.

When the betrayal erupted as illness the first time, she prayed and meditated. Prayer did not stop the longing and meditation was impermanent. When her pain erupted as illness the second time, she frantically wrote in her journal the details of her past, a past in which she was connected to the spirit world, a world of peace and understanding. As a child, and as long as she was alone, her house would team with music. At church angels comforted her as she held silent ears toward the fearful message of the preacher. When the congregation sang of love, lights shined around the heads of the crowd. She wanted only to write about this love. Her journal began uncovering truths about her existence, about her longing for a reconnection to the spirit realm, and a reality of her love being taken for granted. Her pain erupted as a torrent of raw emotion. Her journal began to take the form of her memoir.

Rebecca has been attempting to write herself out of despair, a state in which others would call depression. Although others think she has a problem, Rebecca knows this is a chance to transmute raw emotions into a happier state of existence. She is just beginning to understand that she is a part of the bigger picture, a part of the transformation out of a societal insensitivity and into the acknowledgement that sensitivity is a strength. She does not understand how God could allow such a spiritual, loving person like herself to be handed a life of broken heart after broken heart. But she will. And she will by uncovering every spiritual truth that lies within the depths of her emotions and within the sad song of her current story. And although she won't understand her story fully until she is finished with her memoir, it is each understanding that she acquires through writing that allows her to release her resistance, a wall of beliefs created through a myriads of lifetimes by a myriads of souls.

Perhaps you know a Rebecca.

MICHELLE LUCAS

Dedication

To Rebecca

If you only knew how this story ends,
you wouldn't waste one moment in darkness.

In the Beginning

In the beginning, as an adolescent and before the push for identity squelched hope, I only wanted my son back. This peculiar feeling was so strong that I told my 3rd grade friend on the playground. I said, "I will have a son and then a daughter. I won't be married."

I knew my son's face exactly. I saw him at night.

Nearly twenty years later he was born, saving me from my squelched self, pushing me to be my true self. He is the soul that I repeatedly saw as a child. There is no mistaking that face. I wasn't married but I was in love. At 5 months pregnant with our second child, my love and I married. We gained an extraordinary daughter. But outside pressures of conforming to a superficial world wore out any connections of an internal love with my mate. After years of a stale relationship, where companionship was centered on the television, I wanted true love, to be in love, completely in love. For a moment it happened, and in a moment it disappeared.

My past disappointments gnawed inside my guts. When I was a teenager, I had thought I should become a lawyer or maybe a psychologist. I wanted to stand up for those who had not learned how to help themselves. In an attempt to banish the dramas of my home life and re-create a new life, I enrolled in a psychology school in the northern reaches of Wisconsin, a place whose cold could keep me numb from a distant past. That dream ended before stepping onto campus. Through the words of my family and companions, it was apparent that my small, Deep South world didn't honor psychologists or lawyers. They were shysters. If I didn't go into real medicine, I would look stupid and weak. I was weak, at least emotionally. The idea of looking less than ideal to the people in my little world surpassed my inner calling. I allowed the beliefs of others to change my destiny. I changed my major to biology.

Once I worked as a biologist I met my companion and hoped dearly that he would release me from my job. I constantly yearned to be a Human Rights lawyer. I thought of how happy I would have been, but instead I went down into the muck of an unhappy marriage and it took having my son for me to see my escape out of that self-created life.

Later came a time when I was totally broke. I stopped imagining a happy career because I wanted money more than anything else. It came but only in sporadic spurts, and only when I had inner peace. Otherwise, I felt poor.

Then, a great loneliness snuck into my life as a divorced 30-something. I wanted nothing more than companionship. He appeared as Hugh and left as an ache that would never heal.

And more recently, feeling chained to another deadening job and to the will of others, I begged myself to break free. I've wanted nothing more than freedom.

Hasn't happened. None of it. Instead, I hold onto despair and hopelessness. The same people and circumstances keep appearing in my life, hurting me in repeated waves. I've broken down and gotten back up, again and again. But, there is a limited amount of times that a human can regain strength. There are waves of delight, but the trenches seem much deeper and longer.

I want the inner substance that does not allow this to happen.

I am Rebecca and I haven't found lasting happiness. I don't know from where happiness comes to reside and I don't know what part of myself stops it. My soul tells me that my personality will not win. It is my Inner Self that will one day receive the glory. So it is my Inner Self that I wish to know. Over the years I've wanted many things. What I received was always temporary. I want to know my true desires, the desires of my soul that I believe will bring permanent results. Bit by bit a happy feeling arises as I write and as I meditate. It is here that I find a tiny speck of my soul. Moving within to some hidden light, I feel a potential that could be born. I feel what my Inner Self truly desires. I want to be a spiritual teacher here on Earth, with my son and daughter, writing this book. For a moment I smile and then I open my eyes. A part of me knows, but it is not Rebecca. Perhaps if I just put that hidden light onto paper I can edge closer to happiness.

I know the book will be successful. I know this because of the enthusiasm that envelops me every time I imagine its completion and when I am speaking from my heart's desire, from my spiritual understanding, and how it uplifts me, how it expands me and how it begins owning everything I was and am and ever will be. When I am acting from this place, this essence encapsulates me and my surroundings and all that is, was or ever will be is beautiful.

Radiant. Free. Abundant. Complete.
Grains of sand are everywhere. Grains.
They shift so we shift, too.
They are but memories upon which we stand.
Relax. Information connects the Earth to its wonders.
Pass it on.
Change. Grow. We've all been here before.
The sands are the proof. We remember.
Just a collection of our thoughts dwindled beneath the feet.
This is behind Sara. She lives only in the abundant mind.
Playing in a field of Violet, what can we create?
Such Fun. Such Joy. Such Love.
Pick more violets. Only choose violets.
The field is eternal. Growth is immense. I see joy, I choose it.
Even while in the shadows, play only with the violets.
Minds expands. Life expands. The New arrives. Worlds open up.
Pick violets with your partner. Worlds collide.
New worlds are created.

Memorate

Taking the best from my life, I come to accept that this moment, this place, and this time are good enough. I reckon a distilled end to my story. The train stopped at my finale, a hopeless, insignificant ground. I never imagined this filthy, graffiti-hole as my destination. But, it is here that I came after repeated anguish. My dreams remind me. A lingering stale air and a lonely, reddish structure, blurred by disappointment, stand before me. Halos of thick smoke cling obtrusively and permeate the space that should be open to glow.

Love brought me here. It didn't cure all like promised; love impaled me. Career burdens me, responsibilities weigh me down, and the need to reconcile all the regrets has weakened my body to its lowest.

In my repeated dream at the train stop, I turn and gaze at the tracks of where I've been, wondering how I ended here. I see the waves of lavender in southern France and smell the brusque Icelandic rye. I see my children when they were young and so very happy. I see my son in Florida when he entered a hula-hoop contest and came so very close to winning over those little girls. I remember goodness in the air when cooking with my daughter. I see our smiles. I pause in disbelief of that woman, Rebecca, the one I no longer recognize. Recurring traumas of the heart and simple life struggles now deaden me.

I view my past and see how I resurrected myself many times

by engendering hope into my existence. But in this space, at this train stop, heaviness is exacerbated by a dim, moist air that makes it hard to breathe. My body is tired and my mind dry. The energy to resurrect myself once again, just isn't here. Despair seems to be the final destination.

I have no hope, yet it is my middle name. I can't take the risk of jumping on another potentially sabotaged train. My doubts and beliefs, or disbeliefs, would go with me and the destination would look the same. Rides on toxic love trains are what dump me here repeatedly. I should have jumped off this last one sooner and avoided another heart wrenching disappointment.

DID I DETERMINE THIS DESTINATION, OR WAS IT DETERMINED FOR ME?

Have I been riding along on a pre-destined journey, or did the accumulation of pain become all I know, determining the destination from all of my destitute imaginings? I've become the person who expects to get hurt in the next step, to be demolished if I take a risk and betrayed by the next person, just like the last.

I am alone. My kids are almost grown and have their lives to live. I am unhappy at work and I haven't had a true partner for nearly two decades. But, I do have a story. This story I must tell. Insights on the only true existence, spiritual existence, the deep understanding of Self and the price I've had to pay for these, I must blossom from my soul.

I should explain that I'm probably what you imagine an average 41 year old white woman with dyed-blond hair looks like. I'm average in weight and height, once at 5'5" and possibly now getting shorter, weighing around 125 as I have most of my life. If I put on weight - which is hopefully not, but sometimes is, over 10 pounds - it goes straight to my hips, my child-bearing hips. (Apparently, some men are really drawn to this.) If I were to eat a donut right now, I'd see it on my ass in the morning. But, I can still pull off sexy in tight jeans. I'm happy for that. Flat-ironed-straight past my shoulders, my hair is absent of any flow. It's the hospital blinds dropped for the night, purposeful but looking like all the others. Men have told me that they are drawn to my smile, my bigger-than-life, thin-lipped, toothy smile. If you ask me, it's a horse smile. Thankfully, I adore horses.

If I could be drawn to anything about myself, other than my deeply spiritual nature, it would be my eyes. I'm happy to have inherited my grandpa's piercing blue eyes. If eyes are the gateway to the soul, my soul is the nighttime cerulean ocean, still, intense and waiting to penetrate all that comes within reach. This is the real me, that which either intrigues or frightens people. Nevertheless, it's bound to be unleashed.

Today I begin. I must awaken from this damaging consciousness. Today, a new story begins as I write myself out of this filthy graffiti-hole. An inner wealth of happiness must be possible, as the spirits have shown me so. I hope for a triumph at the end. This story is destined to end in glory, as love is the destination of all. But today I am only a defeated shell of existence. The yolk was removed long ago.

This is my story and this is my journal, a journal so used that the letters 'Reb' are all that remain on the cover. I have been writing it for decades, the same story over and over, with different characters but the same results. I held onto it, in hopes of one day writing a good ending. And today I have nowhere else to turn but to do something different. Instead of letting my life happen and reading about it later, I will write myself out of this deep despair. I only know my new story as it is compelled on pages. And I know how I must start.

This is my unleashing of the abyss of my feelings and the cliffs that I reach through a subtle sense of knowing. In the depths of my love and my longings I sway, trying to connect past to present, cause to effect, God to life. Everything is present at once and there are no bounds when emotion flows.

My spiritual insight and the spirits around me say that there will be glory and happiness soon. 'Soon', to the spirits, may be my next lifetime. But, I must try to write a journey to another destination.

Writing is a simple joy. Writing doesn't require energy reserves that I just don't have any more.

My swaying brings a disjointed life, as are the words in my head. These thoughts disrupt my soul as they do to the words that I place onto paper. My swaying is the space from which I have been creating my life. This must end so I may have a self-determined life. These words must end in a symphony after the pain is unleashed.

Don't cheat. Don't surf to the end. It hasn't been written; it hasn't occurred. But, it must be a triumph. My soul has told me so. Just a few months and maybe, just maybe, I'll be happy and in love. It is now August 2010.

This is my story which goes back decades but started a few short months ago, when a stranger entered my bedroom.

CHAPTER 1
The Haunted

She awoke me mid-dream, in the midst of despair over lost love.

I'm dazed from sleep, not yet aware of the time of day or night. I know that I'm in my bed and that it is dark outside. The Head of Charity peers down at me from the wall above as She always does. *Oh, Raphael.*

Stillness outside, except for the mellow dance of the pecan tree brushing my bedroom window. I wasn't finished sleeping. I'd rather be asleep, because the days are full of sorrow. Yet, here I rest, nose to nose with this woman.

Straddling me, spanning me she hovers. Her knees lock to my own, binding me to the bed, flesh to flesh, both hers and mine. Kneeling, she bends to position her face in front of mine. I can't move.

The monks quietly chant from my CD player that I turned on before falling to sleep. I wanted them to bring me good sleep, a deep sleep that I need for physical recovery. I am awake but unable to move. This isn't a mind-altered vision. I feel her; I see her. This isn't another reality that a drug could induce. It's been a decade since I took Percocet and had frightening visions while lying in this same room.

As I would lie down to sleep in this bed each night, alone in that part of my distant past, I was actually locked in an attic in Victorian England. Dark wooden columns arched and met in crosses not far above my head, under which I laid in a cot a few meters from a small window, in through which the cold swept.

Two women, my keepers, peered down at me, although they were not cruel. I could tell by the look in their eyes. Wearing rose and cream-colored silhouettes with sleeves doubled-back at the wrists, lace meeting at an angle pointing to their elbows, the women had the comfort of being much warmer than I. A flat, knit smock hung loose from my breasts to my ankles. It was the keepers' job to see that I didn't leave. They were not happy with this job, yet it was insisted upon them.

Every time this vision was clear, a terror erupted. I would sit up in this bed, in this home on Rue de Gabriel, and stare at the door knob moving left to right and back again. Someone was outside my bedroom, trying to break in. Someone wanted to harm me.

The tree would scrape my window as if to say, 'You can't jump out this window without being caught." I would look back at the turning door handle, imagining the predator on the other side. My heart beat rapidly out of my chest. I thought I was to die. Who was trying to hurt me and why was I here? Feelings of abandonment and immense vulnerability crested. A sense of being punished for something that I had done was thick. It felt as if I had betrayed a law, a sexual law, and that a ruler had locked me in this attic to keep me from the man that I would otherwise be committing to adultery.

Each night, knowing that death would be my fate if I didn't attack, I grabbed a candlestick larger than a baseball bat, one large enough to kill someone if I hit them right. Then I would leap out of bed and lunge at the door. Each night this leap awoke me and I would be left standing in the open doorway, awake and aware that the door was never shut and that I'm in my bedroom near the Cane River. Heart racing, aware that it was just a dream. A Percocet dream. Perhaps.

But now, this is not a dream. A woman is really here and she yells without moving her lips, "*Wake up, Rebecca!*" Hand slap across the left cheek. No real pain. I'm just startled awake. My eyes try to focus in the dim room, lit only by the full moon sketching the pecan tree on my wall. That Pecan tree sits between my walls and the river and its ghost breaks through the crack in my thick violet curtains. I start to see the details of her face and I'm nearly taking in what is happening. A bird is chirping from a knotted twig of a finger that is scratching my window. It is early morning. I am in my queen bed with curling chrome rails reaching high over my head to Charity.

Through the dampness covering my eyes, I see deep into hers - dark and off-set eyes with deep corners that seem to stretch upward to the hairline. Cleopatra eyes. Her face is slightly flat with smooth, Asian-like transitions and it is a glowing pearl.

Her persistence to bring herself into my awareness comes from love and perhaps some type of duty toward me. Like the sun reflecting off of a crystal blue lake, love radiates from her. Sincerity sings like a harp played by a young, praying child. Trust is her prayer and is exactly what she is willing forth for me to be. Her mind is calm and her thoughts free.

She can hear me speak when I'm only thinking. "Who are you? Why are you here?" A glance of mutual recognition is returned. With a gentle nod to the left, she is asking me the same questions. Her eyes speak of compassion. Her soft, rose-colored lips part in a gesture of releasing my deep-despair. She sees no reason for me to live in such doom. She pauses and waits for my focus and returned understanding.

I'm enamored by her aliveness, her beauty, high cheekbones and tender, sloped nose. Her loveliness is so simple, yet so deep. Undemanding, caramel strands of hair perfectly slide off her cheeks, loosely curling to reach the tip of her ear lobes. Each strand is alive and has never witnessed decay. Her hair has never been dyed. It breathes like the Magnolia bloom catching the sun when lifted by the warm Deep South wind.

Points of light in her eyes reveal internal insight and wisdom.

Her eyes are intense, like mine. I recognize her intuition and passion, because they are exactly what I harbor inside.

But she is different. She's calmer than I am comatose. She's completely self-contained and self-assured. She lives in a space of trust. My space of trust is knowing that the socks I removed last night will be there each morning to maintain the routine of shuffling back downstairs.

ABUNDANCE LIVES THROUGH HER, where worry possesses me.

Even this mystical appearance doesn't lift me from the ache of desolation that I've encompassed for far too long. The keen awareness that I may be destined to aloneness forever is far too apparent to beg for anything more. My day will still be without a partner, without joy and void of the deep love that I recently lost. Even the spirits won't or can't ease me from this anguish. I'm exhausted from the disappointments, and this last one has laid me down.

Like every night, Paul is not lying next to me. I swallow and feel the tightness in my chest where the saliva curls. Through our friendship we fell in love and I've asked him to stay out of my life until he commits to me. He has repeatedly begged me not to run away from him because, as he puts it, "I left my wife years ago. Only the guilt toward my children keeps me from making it final. I will get over the guilt. Things will change for the better." For me, there are no guarantees. None of my past relationships worked. I have been repeatedly let down and why should this be any different? So, I stay distant and in anguish.

The hole in my stomach is surrounded by a vessel ready to crack. Last night, like all the other nights, I stumbled up the stairs with that vessel full of wine, filling that very hole that keeps me more dead than being drunk.

Paul and I were friends for far too long to imagine such a crushing end. I thought that his love for me would release him from his destitute marriage and bring a new chapter to our lives. Instead, he stews in his disappointments as if it is his destiny and clings to me like fingers in a jar of molasses. He gets to taste the sweet idea of happiness with me while I yearn in darkness of not knowing what is to come.

I don't pray as I fall asleep because I no longer believe there is anyone out there to help me. The Reines, whose porch I can view from my 2nd floor balcony, pray to a God who seems to keep their family and spirits alive. Every Sunday morning, the bells of St. Anthony's lay the congregation to rest on the Reines' front lawn. The children play in their Sunday best and the adults laugh and cry with joy, although it all sounds like singing to me. Their union is sustenance. I can see it in their eyes when one of them walks down the street to offer me meat pie. Although there is humble pride in their home cooking, what they are really offering is the sharing of God's love.

What is unclear to me is which ceremony actually creates this sharing of God's love. I hear them talking of the church, Father Floyd, and prayer as that which uplifts and glorifies life to its fullest. It is deep and exuberant love that is expressed. Yet, I'm not certain that it isn't the union, the Reines and their friends, in the moments of laughter in unison and contributions of food to the buffet, that the greatest sharing of God's love isn't practiced.

The Reine's oldest boy, Peter, can sometimes be seen kneeling for a brief moment at the top of the porch stairs before going off to work at Louisiana's oldest general store. The grandeur he portrays as he drops to his knees and his beaming smile prove that he's not asking God for blessings or help through the day. He is blessed. He's thanking God in prayer for having this day.

I let go of that perception years ago. I want help. I want blessings. And maybe this woman is it, although my soul feels so desolate.

She has awakened me mid-dream, where I had just seen her for the first time. Now she's in my bedroom, in my face, yelling, as only a nice spirit could yell, *"Rebecca, wake up! Don't you see the truth? Paul has to spend the rest of his life dealing with the consequences of his divorce. He loves his children and you can give him the space to do what*

5

is best. His heart is filled with love for you. Perceive it from the point of love. Keep love in your heart."

That is much more reassuring than the thoughts that have haunted my mind. These hauntings I journal daily, in an attempt to release them from my mind, from my aching body:

Maybe he's playing me. He's taking my friendship for granted, my tendency to encompass my loves with ever-endearing love, for granted. I'm compassionate and should be the stoke that holds the wheel in place to turn, since he's weak and in a difficult position. I should understand that he loves me and that this will take time. I shouldn't withdraw my love. I should be the rock. But, maybe he's taking advantage of my love. Maybe I'm the one who stopped trusting. He told me that he was getting a divorce years ago before I fell in love. He was lying to me. He's a liar and a cheat. I hate him. He's too weak to face the truth and I'm taking the blow. Maybe Hugh will return. He was a true love. All the others were just fun, until they lied or cheated. Paul lies and cheats.

When would this madness stop, or when would it stop me? Is the madness coming from Paul, the relationship, my allowance of his selfishness, or from me? Now love - the pull of the heart-strings, too painful to detach. Too painful to not detach.

I long for the connection. The connection of the heart. Anything else just isn't worth it.

An overruling sense of loss eats at my core. The emergence of love, sweet happiness, simply snatched away. A cruel joke. I had to finally get away from what he was doing to me. He begged me to stay. I had to tell him "No, stay for what? A lie? Your actions prove your choice."

My love for Paul drew me back to his arms repeatedly. Although my love was sincere, his excuses grew. Looking into his eyes brought peace and a knowing that we belong together. He would hold me and then explain that it just wasn't time yet. And now after completely withdrawing myself from him, he has moved to the corporate offices in Atlanta, Georgia. 600 miles away. What does that say? What circumstance will ever allow us to see each other again? How do I stop this agony of longing? I try to run but my agony does not hide. I think I must break free of ever thinking of him again and I wail in the feeling that the relationship can't be over. I can't breathe.

The slap, the wakeup call wasn't to awake me physically, it was to awaken my mind. *"Rebecca, perceive it from love. Rebecca, don't you know?"* There's a piece of the puzzle missing. There is something that I don't understand.

Consciousness is fading. I barely feel my head hit the pillow. I must fall back to sleep, back to the dream.

CHAPTER 2
The Fall

Fainting unaware. Consciousness slipping away, like the fly caught in the refrigerator. Frozen in Nothingness, yet falling from denseness. Numb, yet complete and at peace.

Disbelief. No bearings. I relinquish my grasp to the ground behind me. Nothing to position myself to surroundings. My bed is still near, but I've lost it. I fall into the deep sleep within, fall.

No wind, no breath. No coldness or warmth to the air. Greenery, pine whipping me as I fall past nature's outstretched arms. I try to open my eyelids, but can't. Backwards I fall past the same cliff on which I stood before Sara woke me. My arms and legs merely hang in the air as gravity pulls. I can't gain the control that I had before; I've diminished. The boundaries have diminished and it is only I.

The deep plunge seems to have no finale. This would mean death to the body. Yet, I'm too exhausted to care. Then poof! Satiating fabric catches my fall like a plush pillow clutching an infant in its humanized folds. My hair squeezes up past my eyes. I'm enveloped in a massive and lavish, red velvet couch. It is the type imaginable only for a proud, impetuous king, yet it massages the curves of my meager body. The canyon lies far beneath while the cliff peak is not too far above.

Moments pass in confusion that takes place in a space separate from my mind. The only thing solid are the pines. I am scared. This couch is perched merely on pine branches. I, on this couch, am in a shaky predicament. I fell into a shaky predicament.

In the beginning of the dream, before I laid awake haunted in bed, I had reached the top of this cliff after conquering a hill of boulders. Those obstacles beneath my feet were difficult to navigate. Yet I trudged up that hill, with stick in hand and a smile on my face, not knowing where it was leading. The climb was tedious with the weight of the backpack bound to my own. But when I reached the top, I could go no further. I had come to the ledge. Sparingly, through clearings in the pine, I could see for miles. Vastness was overwhelmingly before me.

I don't know what made me do it. After reaching the top I stepped out over the cliff onto a thin branch. I was shaking so I held onto another branch above for dear life. Falling from a summit, losing control, is my greatest fear. Balancing, I watched as red rocks scooted over the edge and plummeted to the abyss, dissipating into nothingness. Fear of losing my grasp or unfastening my footing took hold. Looking down only made me weak. At first I couldn't see the bottom of this abyss. Trembling, I looked forward. An unknown world came into view before me while I knew that disintegration fell below. A golden field stretched to the end of the Earth, but it was naked, an empty field holding nothing. It had only the sun in which to bask. A man was to my back urging me to jump. "Jump. Just jump Rebecca! We will catch you."

Even during the dream, I knew what this meant. I recognized the feeling from a previous time. I was being urged to jump into the unknown, which was possible demise to me. I looked down. My laptop, my corporate laptop, fell the full 3,000 foot drop to its death. I had made it go. Left foot in front of the right, I tried to keep my balance on that thin branch. I was so afraid of falling, of jumping. I had done this once before. The landing was not easy; yet, I never regretted it. How could I know that I would land safely this time?

This urge to jump was the same feeling I had when I left my

first job out of college. I hadn't gone far from my home parish, but very far from my Wisconsin college town in which I had wished to stay. Only 45 miles down the highway - to what I describe as an institution – to dwindle my days away in a lab making solutions, analyzing solutions, and reporting data. Staring into vials and rarely into real faces, I lived a sort of death to my soul. I gave it three years before I couldn't take it anymore. Then, I jumped off.

I fell into poverty.

Now again I stand on top of a cliff, realizing my fear of failure. I was just in this realization, standing on top of the cliff, before the slap across the face. The faceless man behind me pointed to the field at our left. I had yet to look in that direction. I had not yet taken in all of my surroundings, all of the distant possibilities. He pointed to a woman, "That is Sara," and noted the beauty in which she lived. She glided through that vast field which was replete of violets. She carried a basket full of the picked flowers and her hair was delicately ornamented with the same. A ring of violet dawned her caramel hair and the source of her beauty was profusely apparent. The field of violets is the field of her perceptions. She chooses to live within this abundant mind. She chooses only beauty; and therefore, she is beauty. I saw her abundance and felt her assurance that she will never be poor. She is rich from her focus on the good things. Happiness permeated her being because she chooses to stand in that field of violet, in the thoughts of glory, and kindness and love. She is radiant.

Violet thoughts make her radiant.

Brushing, yet not disturbing the flowers, she walked, smoothly, calmly, and gracefully. She didn't need to indulge because all she needed was at her disposal. It is where she lives. She reached a tree and sat in a miniature egg of shade. The sun was high overhead bearing light to everything in reach, except this small patch of earth that was nurtured by the tree. From the tree's love, violets grew within its shade.

Sara bent over to put yet another purple flower above her left ear, making a perfect ring of honor around her crown. She chose the beauty before her to adorn herself with the love that connected it all. From the shade she picked a couple more violets to add to her basket and then she sat in silence.

Tim pointed farther left in the field. Most peculiarly, in that space was Paul. He was looking at the ground, eyes directly on the flowers, but not noticing them. He meandered like a lost puppy, not noticing the beauty or the bounty at his feet. Aimlessly, he wandered without picking the flowers. Paul crushed violets beneath his feet, unconsciously of course, although he never looked up from the ground. "Paul is Sara's husband." The faceless man told me. And it was abundantly clear that Sara was happy, even if Paul was crushing violets.

And now swaddled by the velvet fabric, I lie in trepidation. If I bend my left arm, my elbow will be over the edge. The movement might shift the couch throwing me to my death. Sara is over my knees, as if she never left my bed. Faceless Tim sits behind her. Thoughts of rolling over and falling to my death paralyze me. Thoughts of Tim moving and creating the same demise lock me. Yet Sara and Tim are both calm and patiently waiting for me to relax into their understanding. I sink deep into the fabric to find a remnant of safety.

Sara still straddles me as the feeling of surrounding protection seeps into my awareness. But I own my own fear and I own the spinning turmoil that moves from the pit of my stomach up through my heart. No one has control of me, but me. No one has control of the potential fall off of this couch. No one can throw me off.

I weigh the possibilities. If I take the risk of standing up and crawling back up the cliff, I could make a fatal error. The possibility of going left means death. I can't move from this prone position.

And it is Sara, removed from the field of violet, who is here in my face and on this couch, straddling me. Maybe I'm still awake, but I'm so dizzy with the thoughts of falling into the abyss that I cannot distinguish that which is awake from that which is asleep within my mind.

I'll be safe. I won't fall. I can leave my job for the work that I love. I'll jump and I'll land in comfort. I'll trust and jump out of my life of despair. Someone or something, maybe God, maybe Fate, will catch me, just like this couch. "You'll be fine", says Sara. "You will go on to live the life you were meant to live, in love and happiness. Why do you worry? Why do you bring on the emotional storms when the universe provides you with everything you'll ever want or need?" She doesn't need to speak to me through the mind as she did in my bed. I am now in her space. Her lips move. My body may be asleep, yet I am awake. Sara speaks to me directly.

CHAPTER 3
Bare

Bare and sorrowful, I am awake for the day. I slowly open my right eye to view the hazy numbers on the screen of my cell phone. It's 7:12, much later than I usually wake. Stuffed feelings usually stir me around 3:00am. It's rarely a morning that I fall back to sleep after acknowledging the torment of the heart.

I reach for a robe that isn't here. Last night's sweat pants and dingy shirt lay on the floor. My day will begin like all the others. Wobbly legs make it to the bathroom sink so I may brush my teeth. The muscle tone of the once athlete has vanished.

Staring into the mirror that is blemished with soap and makeup, I try to focus. The haze reminds me of the obscurity that occurred last night. *Something good happened last night.* My mind begins to focus on the reality before me while my pupils undulate until I can see through the fog. The energy to wipe the blemishes before me is not here. I can barely see through my accumulations.

My face has hardened recently. My eyes are dim, like my thoughts. The lids are thick and hang like scum on a pond. They haven't been wide open for months. My blue irises are gray and covered in the murkiness that I can't seem to break through. The reflection staring back at me is someone I don't want to know. She's older than what her age tells. The folds across the eyelids are deep and now travel below the temples into the cheeks, revealing accumulated grief. And the skin is so broken, so rough and pale. I rest my elbows on the hard basin and lean closer to the mirror. I'm not steady and I need a moment. *"Where is hope?"* I ask that jaunted face before me. *What day is it? The face responds, "Saturday. It's the day Dora arrives. At least you have something good today, Rebecca. You can spend time with a friend. You rarely get time with your one and only close friend."* The thoughts of Dora open a doorway to remembering my sleep. *Oh dear God, who was that last night? Did that really happen? Who is Sara? Will I really be happy again?"*

I yearn to be touched, to be loved. My stomach churns in fear of disappointment, in dread of betrayal. *But maybe there is hope.* My reflection is horrid, so I backtrack to my bed, returning to enter the same old clothes of last night. I know that I must make today a better one than the last. But, how?

Focus, Rebecca. I must learn to focus on all the good things in my life. This is what I heard last night. A strong message of peace, whether spoken in words or through an energy of a higher mind. *How do I focus on the good when I feel broken? Paul is gone and my corporate job exhausts me. It's not financially possible to leave my job; it's not smart to ask Paul to re-enter my heart.*

Like a tortoise lost in her shell, I pull the heels of my feet underneath me and sit in the darkest spot in my room, back propped against my bed. I want to remember last night clearly; I want to recall the moments when such glory happened in my life. It is somewhat difficult to recall those lost days when I felt so abundant with love of beings on the other side.

Spirits appearing in my dreams, touching my hand, or whispering in my ear wasn't uncommon, although this hasn't happened for many years. There was a time when I slept just to get messages from the spirits. They hovered brightly in awakening vibrations over my left shoulder. Falling to sleep with them, I dreamt in enlightening awareness. They rained into my mind as feelings of being lifted, of being swept away on the wings of a hawk, or moving from one open-air school room to another, going from teacher to teacher to receive offerings. Interpreting my dreams became a second profession. But, then there were those other dreams. Many were foretelling in ways that I didn't want to be revealed. Some messages were clear, as when they spoke boldly through a veil. *"Don't go there, Rebecca,"* when they knew I was well on my way.

Today I have dreams that are easy to interpret, but they don't come from those enlightened beings. They clearly come from my disruptive emotions. Tornados speak to my emotional turmoil, while a dinner buffet lets me know that I will have more money or love soon. It seems I've dreamt of a thousand storms but only of a couple buffets.

Last night broke through my emotions. Sara was physically in my bed and her message was clear. She spoke through her mind when she manifested in front of me, thoughts traveling from her mind to my own. My perceptions are causing me to feel doomed. There's an urge to leave my current life, my current career, as I know it. *I need to drop my corporate job off a 3,000 foot cliff.* Her message told me that love can be mine if I focus on beauty in life. *I'm going to be fine. I'm going to be happy. Everything is going to work out. Damn, I can't possibly imagine that!*

Faith in a higher power and a feeling of being divinely guided used to give me the energy to explore life. When I was only five, angels picked my grandpa up from the floor when he fell out of his pew one Sunday morning. I saw them. I continued to see them many years of my life until despair took over. *Where are they now?* Following this guidance allowed me to take the little risks necessary to enjoy life. Good results from the guidance brought me hope and it was that hope that made me happy, giving me the energy to go to work, to do the dishes, to pick up a new book, to just get through the day. I've lost hope and don't know where to find it. Yet, it is my middle name, now masked behind the fatalism of my reality. Nothing is easy and love doesn't appear. *Where do I find hope?*

Definitely not in life. In God? In lying Paul? In Sara who just appeared from another world?

Until now, this sort of thing, where a spirit physically transcends the ethereal boundaries to wake me from sleep has happened only once. It transpired a decade ago in the midst of my own painful divorce. But, that spirit was not human; it was a horse waking me from a nightmare.

Purging dark streets and hidden alleys I ran in desperation, my terse body disturbing the darkness which encompassed my life. For what seemed like an eternity, I ran to get away from a man who was trying to kill me. In bare feet, dingy pants and a bomber jacket, he chased me while holding his hand high, donning a knife. I was panting and sweating while running for my life. I was certain that this meant death. I rounded a curve and laid waste to the dirt beneath my feet. A horse stable came into view and I was desperate for someone to be there to save me. I didn't slow down on the approach, only leapt through the center and crossed a shot of light that reached out of a stall. I was too scared to recognize the light. I continued in panic and bolted out the other side, leaving this stroke of light. But, it was from that stall, from within the light that the horse leapt. I should have known that he would save me. I should have stopped and noticed when the sun shone through. Instead, I kept fearing and running.

The horse caught up to me, stammering at my back. His hooves and his breath overwhelmed me. Stammering, he caught my backside. I had to turn around or trip face first.

With hooves high in the air, his weight came down in a thunder on my shoulders. I was staring into his wide, dark eyes when my head hit the ground. Death by knife or horse was the dilemma, of which I had no choice. It was over. The pain was over and the running; the terror was over. I succumbed to death by another. My breathing stopped. So I fell and opened my eyes to know the being who would take me.

My eyes were locked on his mouth, which was already touching my face. My eyes followed his long face upward. Then, I could have sworn that I saw him smile. For certain his eyes were smiling. I couldn't completely grasp what I was seeing, but most certainly this magnificent horse's eyes were saying, *"Come on Rebecca, you don't need to be in this fear. Let me wake you from this."*

From chin to hairline his thick, wet tongue lapped my face, waking me from the tremors.

Once awake, lying in bed, out of the 'dream, I wiped the solid saliva from my face with the back of my hand.

This story is true. It is more real than the illusion within I live. Waking that morning with the back of my hand glistening, not knowing if I was disgusted by the spit or enlivened by the love, I sat up in bed in awe. The horse-breath lingered, and I awoke through my darkness which I didn't realize I had been calling myself to exist within.

Now I must begin another day which isn't a beginning at all. I am still being swept off shore into the sea of intense emotions; it's just that sometimes I am awake for it and at other times asleep.

Descending the wood stairs that no longer hide the accumulated dust, unleashes the creaks that are the loudest sounds of life in this house. I approach my kitchen, witnessing the hopelessness in which I've become accustomed - stained flooring, a sink peppered with dirty silverware and magnets strewn across the refrigerator that can no longer hold the faces of my children. If only a joyful event could appear in my day, then perhaps I could find hope. *Dora arrives today. We will laugh.*

I greet my first daily addiction, coffee only seconds before my second addiction, cigarettes. I sit at my computer, which is void of good news, and stare. *Wait. Last night was different, hopeful.* I find the encouragement to sit in the chair near the window, opposite my usual seat at this small kitchen table. I want to recollect last night, to find hope out of the experience. So easily distracted, I peer out the window hoping to see something inspiring, something different. But, from this view, it's the same old pickup truck parked at the same square house colored like saw grass. Tall columns embellish my neighbors' diminutive home in some resemblance of the Oakland Plantation, as if to say, "We are one. We are on this plantation together. We are wealthy landowners despite what you might think."

Everything is the same. Nothing has changed.

I've never known of Sara before. That's a change. I grab my journal knowing that I should write this down. Writing on paper my fears, my feelings, and my disappointments clarifies what is happening to me. Whereas I usually hold captive my feelings locked deep inside, placing them to paper places them in a realm where I can acknowledge and deal with them. The pain is unlocked from a cellar where it would otherwise kill me, but it is not unleashed.

I hold onto my pain like a soldier to his war. I write.

How did I know the man's name is Tim? He never told me his name. Sara was distinct and material, a corporeal existence being defined by her own choice to make herself manifest to me. The slap moved my head to the right. She was physical and she was there in my bed, as a presence to enlighten my world. I never saw Tim's face.

I should be like Sara. I need to learn to be like Sara, to just choose happiness! If I choose thoughts of abundance, I can live in abundance. If I place my attention on all of the gifts that I have been given, my reality can change. If I believe that I have been given all I need, then all I need will be given.

In the past several years I have rarely, if at all, noticed the presence of spiritual assistance, or of God. But, I know that I have protectors or helpers. This has always been clear. I'm not sure why and I'm not sure how. But, I suspect that they reside in a realm through which my soul extends and that they are in fact a part of my soul. Perhaps they appear to remind me of a part of myself, a part of my strength that is a greater part of my Self.

Native Americans often stood by my bed as a child. Once, around the age of 9, as I laid awake in bed with my common insomnia, a Chief and his apprentice appeared in my room. The Chief, with sharply angled cheek bones and unyielding dark eyes, raised his staff and struck it to the ground saying, "You will. Rebecca, you will." After a moment of staring at me, ensuring that I got the message, they just evaporated. The spoken word was power. The power was in the message. I knew without explanation that one day I would take on a spiritual cause. And, without doubt, it would be done. I would not die without this task being completed. The chief has stayed with me over the years. I've seen him several times. His name is Wochea.

In college I met spiritually gifted friends who added beautifully to my experiences. Brian was a very good friend and lover. I could sometimes hear him speak to me in dreams. His mother was a psychic. I met her only once in 1992 and can't forget her poignant vision of Hillary Clinton one day running for President of the United States.

Once, while shooting pool over beers and whisky, I began to tell Brian of one of my grandfather's stories. I started "My grandpa grew up in Virginia and there was this horse..."

Brian interrupted me. I intended to finish that this was a ghost horse. But before I could even hint at this Brian announced, "Oh, yes. That's Robert E. Lee's stallion." We had never spoke of anything remotely 'out there.' This is how I found out Brian's true nature. This recognition of Brian's nature made me infatuated with him. Of course, I did commend him for his accurate telepathy. My grandfather commonly spoke of a magnificent grayish steed whose gallop caught the attention of the entire street. But, as soon as the horse passed by, it disappeared into nothingness.

Morgan was another college friend from the Deep South who brought more spirits into my life. Spending the night at her childhood home, which had a history of hiding slaves, raping slaves and death; it felt like I was in a game of Russian roulette. The voices were loud and objects often changed position on the mantel. Everyone witnessed this except for her father who hated us for mentioning it.

I was at her house the day her 15 year old cat named Tali died. Her mom and brother buried Tali for Morgan, as we both cried. Late that evening her father arrived home with no awareness of the missing cat. No one would have informed this negative, closed-minded man of anything except for the way out the door. But that night, we almost witnessed an opening when he darted out of his office in pure attrition, "I am trying to work. Morgan, get your damn cat out of my office! I keep putting her out the door and somehow she's getting back in. Morgan, come get Tali out of my office, right now!"

Tali was still living after death.

Later I met more spirit guides through Spiritualists and would often venture to see them for myself through deep states of meditation. This became my love, the reason for my existence.

Then, I changed. In my 30s, after losing repeatedly in the game called love, I blamed my losing the game on my calling. My finger pointed at a spiritual pact to prioritize spiritual truth as the reason for my lack in human love. I blamed Wochea; I blamed Jesus; I blamed Love. I blamed God. I separated from these spirit guides. I shut that part of myself down so I would never again have to ponder a path that is predestined. My tumultuous mind made me feel that the spiritual path is a pre-determined path void of partnership. I wanted nothing to do with it. I was lonely. I wanted love in partnership.

But now Sara. Radiant Sara giving me hope in my time of emotional turmoil. She showed me the happiness and abundance in which I can live, if only I were self-contained, picking flowers of beauty and focusing on high thoughts.

I can't be with the man that I love, the man whose love reaches into the depths of my soul. I long for that connection. My love was so deep that being separated from him rips me from the inside out. Some moments the pain is more physical than emotional and my body convulses to vomit some unknown substance from my soul, but the emptiness puts me beyond a point of being able to vomit. I don't know how to handle these feelings. Hopelessness. Questions of 'why?' Anger at him for pursuing me before he was legally divorced, anger at myself for allowing him. *If my mind is hopeful, my feelings will only be crushed.*

I never expected to fall in love with Paul Oakes. He was just a colleague. He was kind and sometimes funny. He was never cultured in the things that I enjoy nor was he excited about any of my interests. He had no desire to leave the corporate world or travel abroad. He spoke about hobbies he would like to try and about places he would love to see. That was the extent of it. He liked staying exactly where he was at. Sitting behind his accountant's desk waiting for the weekend for a round of golf, Paul watched others take off sailing or flying abroad to ski in the Swiss Alps, and he watched them with a silent curiosity, a curiosity which hid a fear. If he were a penguin standing amidst an open sea watching his fellow penguins dive freely into the sustenance, Paul would stay on his rock wondering, 'why not me?"

Paul wouldn't dream of trying sushi. Sushi is my favorite dinner, best savored in some remote Scandinavian town or seaside bungalow. His dining style is chicken fingers and fries. Pure American bar food is where he is most comfortable. And he couldn't possibly understand a longing to leave the security of a career. I can't imagine not longing to leave such a reality. We're from two different worlds. Nevertheless, he became a friend whom I believed I could confide.

I sometimes look back at the 'signs' in which I believed were telling us to be together. Like the first day we met. In an uncommon snow burst I rested my car alongside a road which paralleled the highway. Only five minutes had lapsed when a man, a man who would come to be known as the love of my life, approached to ensure my safety. It was there in that little Louisiana anomaly that he mentioned the company to which he was driving, the same company for which I worked. The second sign was when I fainted in the lobby of our office building immediately after he walked through the doors. I had never fainted in my life and have not since. Lastly, was the evening of 'signs'. These signs were too coincidental. I thought the coincidence meant an appeal between our souls. Yet now I wonder why I didn't I see the signs of destruction.

Well down the highway and on my way home, I realized I

had left a credit card on top of my work desk. I called work. Paul answered. I hoped that my desk was unlocked for him to hide my credit card. At that very moment, heading toward me, end over end, came a truck from the opposite side of the highway. I was in a construction zone, locked in by small walls of cement with trucks to my front and back. After tumbling nose over tail about three times straight at me, the truck came to a rest upside down, mere yards from me. I hung up with Paul to call 911. Minutes later Paul called back to confirm he had my credit card and was unable to lock my desk. I would have to get the credit card directly from him. As he stared out of the office window talking to me, lightning struck just beneath, sending crackling echoes through him, through the phone and into my ear and cheek.

A year later lightning struck when Paul grabbed my hand while strolling down Front Street. I can't explain the feeling completely because it came from somewhere so deep, from a recess of my being that I had yet to discover. It was warmth and comfort, healing and love. It rose from the pit of my stomach as a balloon slowly letting out its life to the vastness surrounding it. It felt like love was released into my heart.

He didn't really explain himself and I didn't really ask. I should have asked. He had announced years prior that he was going through a divorce. It must have been complete. But, I didn't ask that day on Front Street. Instead of asking, I let the feelings take over. Feelings light as a feather. It felt like love that I couldn't deny. I had been waiting decades.

Since love took hold, life has taken its toll on me. Paul later confirmed that he was still in the middle of the divorce. His own family sufferings were behind the delay. His young daughter's illness, leukemia, so rare so tragic. His wife's car accident soon after the diagnosis. The bills were adding up. Levels of grief laid one on top of the other. How could I pressure him to be with me amongst so much uncontrollable grief? So, I waited. When I loved him, I feared that he would leave, a fear so painful that I couldn't face him. When

I separated from his love, despair made all of the decisions. And now he has left.

I should have imagined. After a year of idealizing this great life that we would create, my eyes are opening to the truth, to his lies. He could not have fled his family and moved to Atlanta. He could not truly love me and yet make a decision to separate himself from me.

God could cradle my face right now and say, "Rebecca, you are dearly loved and you will have all of the love that you ever want or need" and I would still be staring into this ash tray. I don't believe it. I've been blessed with wonderful, healthy children and with being alive. But, life is dim because I've been sacrificed by love over and over. I've sacrificed myself for another man's wishes too many times. I'm left with numbness.

I wish I were like Sara, self-assured, confident, in love with life. Since Paul was standing in that same field of violet, does that mean we want the same thing? Are our souls together in another dimension? Is this why my soul feels pulled toward Paul? Tim said Paul is Sara's husband. What does that mean? How can I become like Sara, the self-contained Sara who was unaffected by Paul's doings? I can be happy. I'm blessed to have received spiritual insight last night and I should be happy.

But now I'm crudely awake with my coffee and cigarette and the same worries are present. I only need to call on them. I'm still deadened, like most mornings, wondering if Paul will ever return or if there is another relationship out there for me somewhere. Just being awake allows me to call on my worries. Will this dizzying realization of loss ever leave? Is there any hope? Paul is gone. My love is gone.

But last night was different. A woman in my bed. She was trying to make me see a better point of view. I must understand why I'm so lost, so sad, in such despair with the belief that life won't get better. This grief over love, I've experienced too many times.

I feverishly regret the love that I spoiled on Paul.

I reluctantly make my way back upstairs to shower, in preparation for Dora's arrival. We will do our typical, not-much- of-anything day. But, at some point we'll make it into town and I must be presentable.

She's early. I've barely made it out of the shower and I can hear her voice stretching across the lawn outside. With a towel on my head, I've yet to make it to my underwear drawer, but I open the old window anyways. A wheat penny sits on the pane.

"Dora! The door is unlocked. I'll be down in a few minutes." I yell into the lawn. Petit Isadora has the quiet presence of a jaguar in the night jungle, but the roar of a lion. And that skinny 5'2" Tennessean gal has the opinions of a hawk lunging in for the kill. 'It's mine for the taking.' She's a riddle. She locks herself up at home, without motivation to wonder outside. She'd rather be alone than having attention placed on her and she definitely roars if someone attempts to take her picture. Yet, in every conversation, she invariably calls all the notice to herself like a fly zapped on a violet light. She puts the grocery self-checkout machines into a different language to then complain that she can't read the screen. And when faced with a professional decision in a township meeting, she pulls out Tarot cards. In fact, she loves everything esoteric, from fortune tellers to dowsing rods and ghost hunting, she's got it all covered. Yet, she won't allow good attention to be placed on her. She is afraid of friendship.

Recently she called the attention of the police. She came home to sadly find an injured dog lying in the middle of her cul-de-sac. Frantically screaming, she ran into her house and instructed her boyfriend to call 911. "Hit and run! Hit and run! Call 911!"

Coming to the rescue, Lee quickly went into gear and called 911. He explained to the operator exactly what Dora was describing. "There was a hit and run. A man is injured, lying in the middle of the road." The operator called for dispatch to the area. Lee relayed the operator's questions and instructions to Dora. "What is he doing right now?"

"He's lying there and he can't move! Tell them to get the ambulance here immediately!" Dora screamed back

"An ambulance is on its way," Lee continued, jumping to the closet to get supplies. "It's getting dark."

While retrieving the goods, Dora was screaming about the bastard that could hit this poor soul and run off, all the while the dogs owners were saving the sweet pooch.

"Do you see him, Dora? Let's run."

"He's still lying there, alone, in the middle of the road."

"He's alone, mam," Lee explained to the operator as they ran downstairs.

"He's yapping so sadly," Dora belted as they reached the front door.

"Yapping?"

"Yes, yapping. What do you think he'd be doing? He's in pain!"

By this time the dog's owners were staring Lee in the face as the lights of the ambulance neared.

"The poor thing. Hit and run!" Dora exclaimed angrily as Lee wondered about his inability to read this woman he's lived with for a decade.

Happily, the dog survived with just some time in a cast.

Dora and I met soon after our respective husbands had ended our marriages. We were the only two women to attend a tantra workshop without partners. We had both chosen to endure Madison, Wisconsin's bitter February cold to attend a spiritually erotic exercise alone. This is supposed to be synergistic training, where the total effect of the combined forces of love, is greater than the sum of the parts. Yet, there we were, alone and hopeful that someday we could put it into practice. We were the only ones to pursue the trainer for conversation over lunch and it was there that we began to know one another, and laugh.

Now, a year since I visited her in the Smoky Mountains, she is here for her first visit at my home. The fact that she drove over 400 miles to support me is a testament to our friendship. It's clearly due to my anguish that she has come, to attempt to part me from this pain.

"Rebecca, I'm disturbed by the look on your face. I've never seen you so miserable. It shows in your face, in your eyes. Please stay away from this man. I don't ever want to see you hurt like this again."

"But, Dora, I can't explain it. I can't make sense of it mentally. I have a thousand reasons not to love this man, but my heart and my gut are pulling me. I can't stop remembering the love that we shared and something deep pulls me toward him."

I've never seen such a look of caring on her face, as we sit on the front porch oblivious to the neighbors, to our surroundings, to the heat and the storm that is approaching.

Dora has a big heart, but bears mostly curse words. She doesn't accept the reality that humans have created and eagerly will tell a stranger her hatred of his opinion.

At least our hearts have a similar appeal. If in a circumstance of saving life, we feel we would both save an animal before saving a human. We've often pondered the origin of this. I suspect that it's due to the recognition of the animal's vulnerability in this world humans have largely taken over. Humans have the power to take away the buffalos' land, the cat's food, and the eagle's nest. We can turn our eyes from the dog that is to be euthanized because no one wants him. Yet, except for the young child, humans have the resources to delay their executions.

Dora and I reach out to the most vulnerable, the most helpless. This vulnerability we must each harbor deep inside. It scares us. We don't know how to heal it, so we sow our hearts to others with the same vulnerability and try to heal them. Social work for abused children is her profession. Although she turns a deaf-ear, I've expressed repeatedly that the assistance she gives these children helps heal her own fears of vulnerability.

"Dora, I had a most telling dream recently, a different dream than the one with Sara. I disembarked a train in New York City after coming from a cocktail party with my colleagues. I slowly looked up to the top of the skyscraper next to me that was lit up on the top. Then, I got on a second train that was hooked to concrete. As soon as it started to leave the station, and started to be decimated by the pull of the hook, a man appeared behind me and told me to jump. He kept screaming at me to jump. I jumped off the back of the train, and instead of landing in the station, I fell into Nepal. I walked down a hillside that was covered with Nepalese people, very happy Nepalese people. Oddly enough, they were eating spaghetti. At the bottom of the hill, I bought a 3- foot submarine sandwich in the midst of a man playing a violin and a mass of people praying. I tried to purchase a souvenir, but the man at the booth handed me a book on love."

"Rebecca, you must listen to that dream! Dreams about skyscrapers are your Higher Self speaking to you! You need to write that book you are always talking about. That's what the dream was telling you."

"Dora, I felt like the train was sabotaged. I was scared that I was getting on the wrong train. Am I sabotaging myself, Dora? Do you think jumping off this love train and out of my stressful job will actually save me?"

"First, you are sabotaging yourself by giving your power to Paul. His inability to commit keeps you feeling helpless, which heightens your emotions. Your emotions make you weak because your energy is going to thinking about Paul and what he'll do next! Second, your Higher Self is making sure that you don't like your job and that you aren't happy with your relationships. If you liked your job and everything was easy, you would have no reason to follow your inner guidance, an inner guidance that will take you to your purpose where life is simpler and work does not feel like work."

"But I believe that Paul truly loves me. Do you think he's trying to control me?"

"He's unconsciously trying to control you. Your energy makes him feel better. But this is not what matters. Rebecca, your dream ended with a book of love and that is after you jumped off of the train! Maybe you will write a book on love. There is one thing that I do know, you aren't doing your life's work! You aren't living your passion like you did before entering the corporate world. You keep getting on the same train, with the wrong job and the wrong man."

"I know you are right. I spend too much energy watching my back at work to stay away from the sharks. My energy is depleted and perhaps this is the cause. I no longer know where to go."

"You keep picking the wrong man and feel doomed by the disappointments. You wasted your precious energy on pleasing Paul and now he is gone. You could have been writing!" Dora implores me to understand. "How about a stroll?"

"Sounds great. We both could use a little fresh air," I answer.

Off we go the several blocks to Front Street, cigarettes in hand. After a heavy lunch of white fish augrautin and craw-fish ala-mode, we make it to the river side to lie in the grass and digest.

"Let me read the clouds for you. I'll see a message for you and Paul," Dora playfully says.

I look to the sky and see only white puffs of cotton, some turning gray and growing while turning under, gathering themselves. But, Dora, now she sees it all from a different perspective.

"I see an elephant. Yes, it's an elephant. Do you see it? Paul is an elephant. He remembers something that has scared him or hurt him and he's playing it out again, as if it's all he knows. He's fearful that the pain will be repeated."

Burden's shift away from the sands.
You can witness their relaxing.
Especially in the silence of the night
Is there any greater silence than the
midnight wave crashing to shore?

It breaks the touch, waves through the skin
Visions so clear tasting heaven's vigor,
Excited to be alive even when the world is not looking.

Breathe.

No sounds hear. Hear only no silence.
Here you are complete, already, although you don't believe it.

In this silence hitting the sands, you float
Outside, tomorrow, you play.

SARA

CHAPTER 4

Buried

December 24, 2010. Please God, tell me how to get my life back. I can barely move. I feel so alone. My body is numb with grief. It's been the same relationship, failed and doomed, over and over. Most of my energy goes to working and to paying the bills. I just want a little joy and companionship in my life. My broken heart has left me in what feels like ruin. How can it be that I'm spending another Christmas without a companion? When will things get better?

My journal is all I have today. I thought life would get easier since Dora's loving visit. Instead, Paul's continuous e-mails haunt me. He says he loves me, that he will be frequenting our Louisiana offices and hopes to spend time with me. I do not respond. If I open my heart to him, it will surely break again.

I have a pattern of running away. The fear of pain makes me not face a person who has hurt me. I shrink into non-existence every time that fear takes over. I haven't learned to be stronger on the inside, yet that is exactly what my soul tells me to do. The grief keeps me from putting it into practice.

I realize that I must face him, face Paul. I must let love in and let love be free without attachment. All of my attachments must be breaking, for the pain I feel today is inexhaustible. Relaxing in the knowing that an inner love flows for him, I feel more at peace.

Letting loose the love in my heart heals the activity that causes my body to ache. I know that love must be the only path, for it is the human destiny, and this knowing commands my mind to align in peace.

March 1, 2011: I want to sleep, just sleep. I want to stop thinking, stop feeling. What does it take to lie on this couch in peace? The love that I experienced made me healthy, vibrant and happy. My insides sang. Why does he not break down every door to get to me? How could anyone not choose love?

Sitting on this same hard, kitchen chair, life has worsened. I am very ill. It's my 6th week of shingles. Shingles in the eyeball. It's my sixth week of sleep deprivation, amounting to, at most, three hours of sleep each night. Shingles, which are damaging my left cornea and causing migraines, bring sheering, heated twinges across my scalp, forehead, and the temple of my left eye. This pain has swelled from the recesses of grief onto the surface of my being.

I've eaten little yet my stomach is in knots. I cry. Writing in my journal is the only contact that I have, contact with myself. I write in the dark since my eye convulses in the light. It starts somewhere in a nerve behind my nose and travels through my temple, up my forehead into my skull and down the back of my neck. Lashes of heat make my eyebrow stand on end. The pain is so intense and focused on this receptive side of my body that the right side of my body isn't aware. I can journal for only a few minutes before I lie back down on the couch.

He said he loved me and fell into my arms crying, pleading that I give him a chance. He said that his separation has been legal for two years while tears flowed down his cheeks. I changed my behavior from distrust to trust. I gave him a chance… again. I thought trust was of the strong, was of God. I'm not strong. Where is God? I brought trust in my heart to provide an opening for love. I haven't trusted for over a decade.

31

I thought that this distrust was my failure. It was not. I shouldn't easily give my trust. Where are my boundaries?

I think of my office that I must return to tomorrow and the light above my desk. I realize that I cannot compete at work; the pain wins over the ability to think. I don't know where I'll find the energy to shower in the morning. But, the physical pain and exhaustion is modest in comparison to my hardened, emotional aching. My dear, sweet children I have seen little. Noise exacerbates the flares. The need to protect my children from my disappointments, from witnessing the hopelessness, prevails. I can't hide it. They will try to comfort me, partaking in my illusion and more easily recreate it in their own lives. If they learn lack now, and see their mother unwilling to fight, hopelessness will be a part of their existence.

He promised that he would be honest.

With this recollection of the hope, the scalpel tears across my eye. Happiness no longer resides in that love. Instead, it tears at my gut, in the place where longing lies. The grieving undermines the slashing in my head. I think of the relationship and the fiery pain soars.

I try to give us hope, that perhaps he'll wake up, return to me as a sincere person. But, the fear of more disappointment rips me apart greater than the grief.

I try to push good thoughts into my mind that I'll find the right person and be happy, and I just cry. It's not the ending in which I attached the core of my being. Every thought tears emotionally and signals my nerves to act accordingly.

Or, is it the emotion that commands my nerves?

In this moment on the couch, my mind, my body and my emotions are acting as one. One cannot hurt without the other. My mind cannot worry without the rest bleeding. My heart cannot bleed without my skin ripping.

It is obvious why this virus exploded into my consciousness after lying in my nerves for 3 decades. My entire physical system has been taxed from riding on my emotional roller coaster. I followed my heart back into Paul's arms when he said that we were meant to spend our lives together. Relief fell from my head to my toes. I melted in bliss. Tears let loose over the blessing of having a good ending to a long, grueling wait. I loved him completely, and completely I gave him my love. I forgave him for the past, I opened my heart to love and opened my soul to a good ending. For two weeks.

Six weeks ago, Paul left on a supposed business trip to the lonely outskirts of cold Flint, Michigan with the rest of the accounting team from work. When it was time for him to travel home, I called him to issue my love and state my excitement to see him over the weekend. The background noise overtook his weakling words. The static in his voice told the truth. I heard the voices of his daughters, the ocean and seagulls. Why would he lie? My faith was extinguished. I didn't have to ask. I hung up and fell to the floor. I vomited, finally. I gagged and heaved in disbelief. That long-worn dread of betrayal in my heart became reality. It took only 24 hours of emotional suffering to awaken with a swollen left eye. The virus re-awoke.

In my time with anguish, I've tried to accept that this relationship was a mirage and that a love ever-after is not sewn in my life. I just can't begin to digest the load of my love taken for granted. My nerves have now unleashed the devil.

Devilish thoughts pervade my body. It is near springtime and the weather outside is perfect. Yet, I remain prone in a blanket with my face stuffed into cushions. How do I stop these thoughts? How do I stop replaying the betrayal in my mind?

I don't know from where the worries emanate, but I know where they come to rest. Not a single nerve of my body is at rest. Full-blown anxiety explodes as shaking and itching and pain. This conclusion must be from a myriad of deep and substantial worries. My body is screaming to put this to rest. I want to rest, but I awake minutes into a nap. I awake with sharp itching on my forehead with absolutely nothing there except the resurrection of an emotional pain. I scratch and scratch, but there is nothing on the skin to itch.

I have never been so aware of how intensely my nerves

communicate my thoughts to the body. My belief in following the heart is smacked back with my reality. Forgiveness is at war with the anger in my mind. My body won't accept the concept of forgiveness. Its pain says to never trust another person again. It is repulsed by intimacy now that it was shared and betrayed.

The mind and nerves do not distinguish the difference between creating from love or from fear. They spark exactly as my subconscious tells them. These feelings of betrayal have lain for decades within my subconscious and I am now acutely aware. Now aware, I have only one choice but to release this pain, this false identity. It must die. Where inside of myself do I believe in betrayal?

I am 42 years old and I've yet to find the path to happiness. Love has taken me to the heights and then to the depths of grief. I keep searching for love to make me happy, but the elation in love is never worth its death. The fatality doesn't happen in sleep. Anais Nin said, "Love never dies a natural death. It dies of blindness and errors and betrayals. It dies of illness and wounds, it dies of weariness, of witherings, of tarnishings." To me, it feels like drowning. There is an initial desperate struggle, but in love, we are reluctant to let go of the struggle and surrender to a peace that we can find within.

I thought that I found true love and true happiness a few times. It's funny how at the time the object of your affection can be everything and All Things. We cannot imagine love dying or the attraction fading. But then, we look back. We look back from the eyes of this new person we've become and that past person just doesn't fit in anymore.

I'm not a new person yet. I'm stuck in this pain that won't stop haunting.

I was crazy in love with my college boyfriend. I could have loved him forever. Through my early college years, I maintained spiritual dreams and desires, since the meetings with the spirits continued to occur at my bedside. I wanted to be their voice for others because their dreams for humanity were much better than our own. However, I wasn't developed enough to secure them into my reality. The contradiction between their understanding and the reality of our human world was such a grand divide that without Brian my mind would have exploded. Brian kept me grounded. He kept me solid to get through college while all along I was living in two different worlds. With Brian I began learning how to reach for what I believed I could achieve. Getting through biology, which was not congruent with my passion, was only one area that our relationship secured for me. That grounding proved essential in knowing my next steps. We served our purpose together. The soul-contract ended, along with the attraction. No going back.

Yet, the love had encompassed us both and I've wanted to repeat that love. *Maybe this circumstance with Paul is a soul-contract to get me to a place in which I am currently unaware.* I've sacrificed myself for love too many times. I've sacrificed being alive for a man. It's time to search for me. I'll reach for my passions. I'll reach for the place I truly wish to live, Colorado. I'll reach to devote my life to spiritual teachings again in an attempt to ignore the painful itching on my face.

Does analyzing my behavior actually heal or changing my behavior ever mend?

The fact that I gave men my attentiveness, my caring, and sometimes my heart without asking for the same in return, and especially never getting the same respect in return, must mean that sacrifice can be a habit.

With sacrificial goat's blood in my aura, it's a wonder I ever reached such insightful peace in my twenties.

Chronic back pain led me to yoga at the age of 21. Yoga led to meditation, which opened me to some stark realizations. The first eye-opener was that meditation was not about seeing spirits, although this was exactly what was happening to me. It was the presence of those spirits that removed my back pain, permanently, yet the other participants in the meditation groups had no interest in the spirits. I could not understand why others did not react to all of the participation. The 'ah-ha' moment came at the age of 23.

My meditation group was unshaken by all of the spiritual activity in the room. I became quite emotional with all of the spiritual help, not-to-mention the loved ones that showed up from the 'other side'. I got agitated by the fact that no one else was responding. Emotions were not present in any other participant other than myself, the facilitator. A woman walked from across the room to comfort me by laying her hand on my shoulder and explained that my emotions are my connection to spirit. She said that I should be proud of being fearless of this deep sensitivity and that she wished she could unleash herself in this emotional way to also experience spirit.

Could it be that part of my plan is to be sensitive so that I'm aware of subtle energies of spirit? Could it be that my emotional responses to Paul give me the option of connecting to spirit? Could it be that this relationship is the one that will finally return me to my passions?

That lady's kind gesture brought to mind a dramatic moment from my past, at 17 years of age. I was in Rome, Italy at the Roman Coliseum with classmates for a one-and-only Latin Club trip abroad. The air was heavy with animosity. Cries for violence escaped from every crevice. My stomach boiled; my flesh crawled. I couldn't exit quick enough to escape the human condition. I expected my friends to be running away, the same as I. Instead, my friends were excited and didn't want to leave the atrocity. A few friends spurted inspiringly vivid descriptions of the vast beauty of the place. I was disgusted by their insensitivity. My friendship with those few were over. To this day, I cannot think of one of those classmates, that classmate who was particularly in love with the place, without my stomach squeezing. But, it wasn't until the age of 23, in that meditation group, that I got the 'ah-ha'. It was only me who experienced a fierce resistance to that coliseum. My classmates weren't being insensitive; it was me who was ultra-sensitive.

Later, my son was born and my love for him ignited my passion to love all of life. Meditation became much more than a pastime. I began leading meditation groups multiple times a week. I taught people to find their spirit guides, to see them or feel them. I began asking my guides questions that my clients posed and I began getting responses. Living in this realm magnetized me to people who desperately needed answers.

"Why did the love of my life, who I met only a year ago, die in an airplane crash?" "Where do I go to get rid of this depression, to get rid of these drugs?" "Will my babies survive?" These were just a few of the heart-wrenching questions that I received. Many of the questions were too painful to even ponder, so I couldn't ask my guides. But all of this awareness placed in another realm, made me different than I had ever imagined.

Some moments felt as if I were one of these guides. I felt it in my face where they would emerge as heat in my left eye and a whisper in my left ear. I took it farther by trying to become them. I tried it out on an unsuspecting group of visitors. I was talking about how to calm your mind and access good feelings, but at the same time, I was thinking horse, feeling horse and trying to become a horse. I concentrated on my face, on my jaw, and imagined it extending. I felt a mane. I felt my long face and my large eyes.

A man jumped out of chair, screamed, pointed and said, "You just turned into a horse!"

That's all I needed. I could do it. I apologized, but with a big grin across my face.

Then, a second pregnancy and I immediately told everyone, "Her name is Marisha." She had been my side during meditation, as Lisa, one of the participants, had seen. Who else would this new, glowing soul have been but my future daughter? The flow of my life had continued, just as I predicted in third grade. I had no doubt, but I did meet resistance. Only my meditation group believed me that my unborn child was a girl. It was that group that brought all pink items to my baby shower; and, it was my family who brought clothes of only blue, green and red. My beliefs agitated them. My differences disturbed their reality. My certainty made them my grand inquisitors. Their inquisition brought on my resistance. Six months later Marisha was born and my life was complete.

Could it be that Paul is sincere that he wants a life with me some day? Could it be that I stopped moving with the flow of life, with the flow of spirit?

Love was complete. Later, I couldn't understand the complaints from a large portion of my ever-growing meditation groups. They wanted a love-life. They wanted to know how to find their soul mate. At that single time in my life, these questions drove me crazy.

"Connect to God!" I would say. "You'll have a never-ending source of Love that will fill you with more happiness than any human being." I felt God's love day and night and it inspired me. I understood love. Love is the presence of our Spirits inhabiting our bodies. "Be present and you will be love!"

I guess the corporate world has really re-engineered my consciousness to forget this crucial state of being.

I kept going. My aura kept growing. I could feel an inner blaze extending out of me. Once, when walking into a bookstore, I passed a woman who upon noticing me, turned around and followed me to the back of the store. I leafed through a book with her standing behind me, staring at me. I could feel her, but I didn't want to look. Finally she said, "Mam, who are you?" I answered "Rebecca Hope." She said, "No, I mean who ARE you? I felt your energy when you passed me. It brought tears to my eyes. I felt God's love come to me. So, who are you?"

I could not answer, for I did not have the answer. Yet, I did know that I had been breathing in life force for years.

I took God's love to only one firewalk before I began leading them myself. The first time I walked the fire was with a group of experienced firewalkers who were still waiting for the flames to descend to a red-hot glow of coals when I jumped right onto the fire. I walked slowly and deliberately the eighteen feet without a burn. I was exhilarated and liberated from my fears. I could make any life that I wanted.

Even living in this essence of strength and enlightenment, attracting people like myself, I didn't attract a human love-ever-after.

Firewalking turned into motivational speaking which then became spiritual seminars. Yet, no real relationship. But I had love, ever-lasting, all-inspiring love from the heart of all existence. God. I knew this to be true because of the enormous sense of peace and guidance I lived with every day.

Then, I met my soul mate. He damaged my heart more than I could conceive possible. Our love was all-consuming; it fell to the depths of my being and escaped as tears. We knew each other for years before admitting our feelings. He was about to take marriage vows. My husband had just ended ours. He was the same beam of light that I was projecting. Our eyes first met in an auditorium hosting a psychic fair and we recognized each other immediately. The thought, "Why isn't that man with me?" immediately came to my mind. Years later, he told me that at that same moment he asked himself, "Why haven't I seen this woman until now? She is the one."

How could the universe and a compassionate God keep us apart?

The sexual intimacy was a spiraling, convulsing heat of pure love that only wanted to inspire each other and melt together. The relationship was the most intense sexual intimacy of my life, yet we never had intercourse. He did not want to hurt his future wife. The relationship took place on the same plane of existence as my alternate reality. The bonding was taking place on a level of loving desire that could not be replaced.

My left eye would uncontrollably twitch the moment before he called me. *The same left eye that has twitches each time Paul reaches out to me, and the same left eye that is now burdened with fire.* We talked in our dreams. He would touch my arm and my knees would break. Loving him, I would sing in the shower and he would hear my song 10 miles away. We could never hurt each other. But, we did.

The love took his thoughts away from his future wife and away from her children that soon he would take as his own. I couldn't break from this dimension, in which I was completely absorbed, and remain sane. Emotionally and mentally, I broke.

I made sure that his family found out.

The pain did not end there. Instead, it unleashed itself into every part of my existence.

It started as utter disbelief that God would allow true love to be separated. But, it was true. My love was gone and I did not know who or what to blame. As day wore upon day without Hugh and without any recognition of hope, a pain set in. That realization of the separation tore me to pieces in the pit of my gut, causing every kind of acidic reaction imaginable to occur in my body. Brushing my teeth was a nightmare because canker sores filled my mouth. Many foods became indigestible and eating elicited pains that felt like knives ripping my stomach.

But, it was the unseen, deep pain that created the big nightmare. I stopped sleeping for the most part. But when I did sleep, there was nothing but disturbance of mind. Panthers stalked me, snakes climbed on my stomach and tarantulas gnawed at my face. It felt as if I was never in my skin.

I refused to detach from the separation that I felt. What once was a love for God became anger for the separation from Hugh. As I swam in the pain, I became more and more separated until my body was left without the One who nourishes it. I am realizing this now. My body is showing me what happened. But, a decade ago, I only focused on the disruption in my outside world.

My internal divide crushed my external world. I crushed my foot simply moving furniture. The simple operation was done by a surgeon from the 'old school' who did not believe in pain medication during surgery. I awoke to unfathomable pain and my mind protected me by making me repeatedly fall unconscious. The pain was confounded when an infection resulted from the surgery. The entire right side of my body shut down and I could not raise my right arm to hug my children, stir a pot of soup or open a door. Once in the hospital, the intravenous morphine seemed to do nothing. I was in too much pain to scream at the nurses for more pain killers.

Shutting out the raw pain allows for temporary peace, but without releasing the energy, the pain reemerges in an alternate form.

I was told that the strong antibiotics would remove the infection and that the infection would not return.

Two years later the infection returned, and with a vengeance. Again, I could not use the right side of my body and again a yellow puss protruded from a tiny hole in my skin where a metal rod had previously held my bones together. In a panic, the doctor decided to slice open the foot and called for anesthesia. But, in his panic, he sliced open my foot before the intern had applied the Novocain.

As I feel the scalpel of nervous heat shoot across my left eye today, it hardly compares to that few seconds of the doctor's scalpel down the side of my foot.

Painful events continued in my life, and most regretfully, in the lives of my children. Maybe the several broken bones and bruised emotions are commonplace for a high energy boy, but the crushing illness that my daughter lived was the lowest of our lives. After years of extreme tiredness and many visits to the doctor and hospital, Marisha finally showed a symptom that led to a diagnoses of her illness. She was limping as she chased some neighbor boys in a game of hide-and-go-seek. I called out the window for the cause of this limp and she described a terrible pain in her hip. She explained that it had been there for a very long time. It was only after the biopsy and the surgeon's description of her bones that we realized Marisha's high tolerance for pain. The next seven days were the worst of my life. They had given Marisha a 99% chance of bone cancer. Day 5, the day we expected the results, came and went. I couldn't believe that 'no news is good news', it must have been worse than expected, although I continually heard spirit say that it wasn't true. On day 7 we got the call that the results were unexplainable, since the tumors in her bones could not be the result of anything but cancer. She went in for more tests, at which time she was in a wheel chair due to the pain from the tearing away of the muscles and ligaments from the pelvic bone. After weeks of confusion and fear, a rheumatologist took Marisha as a patient, believing her illness to be a rare cousin to arthritis. And indeed, it was.

I, like any other loving mother, would take Marisha's pain to relieve her of it. I wish I could have taken it all away, the disease, the thousand needles, the medication and the fear.

Contingent with the multitude of devastations occurring, my own body kept breaking with illness after illness. Then my children's father moved forty miles away to the parish of his new wife's family. Coincidentally, their home was only ten minutes from the hospital where Marisha was receiving weekly treatment and rested in a school district that was regarded as the best in the state. Since my ex-husband had the money to give our children everything they needed, and I did not, I allowed his new home to be my children's home. A decision that would leave me more shaken and alone. Buried in pain, I could not see a reason to trust God again.

And now, after a decade of not trusting, I am broke. I am not just sad or living in a dreary time of my life. On a gray, dreary winter day, I can see the swaying reflections of the magnolia trees in the muddy river. Not today. I am buried in the night.

CHAPTER 5
Unfinished Business

I shove my face into the hard pillow and surrender myself to this couch. I can't breathe. I need help. I need hope.

My now 15-year old daughter Marisha helped me last night. She took me out to the movies to see "*Eat, Pray, Love.*" It was Marisha who first told me about the book and movie many months ago, if I had only listened to her at that time. She had said "Mom, there's a book about a woman who is like you. She likes to travel and meditate just like you. You really need to see the movie when it comes out. I think it will make you feel better."

So last night, partially as an attempt to resemble some sort of normalcy in my life, I allowed my daughter to take the lead on what would give her mother hope. I recently read the book but my mind was too dull to allow it to shift me. But oh, what an inspirational ending. In the final pages Elizabeth Gilbert speaks of the Zen, saying that the tree calls forth the acorn. The oak "wants so badly to exist that it pulls the acorn into being, drawing the seedling forth with longing out of the void."

I know this to be true. I saw this in both my near-death-experience and in my clients when I gave them readings in my 20's. All suffering is from not recognizing the Divine within. That Divine part of our souls is pushing to be born. But it has to push through our fears and our useless desires just to be expressed. That pushing feels like pain, whether emotional, mental or physical because these things are blocks to the Divine and they show themselves in a myriad of forms until we release them. My daughter blessed me last night by reminding me to surrender and follow the inner desire.

Liz Gilbert's ending completes my beginning, it pulls me forth. I always wanted to write. Thoughts of creating my own book pop into my painful skull, still overwhelmed with scorching shingles from nose to eyebrow, from left eyeball to crown and from scalp down to neck.

The light from the computer is too bright for my eyeball. Writing a book at this moment is impossible. Yet, this morning is a little different. Marisha's love changed things. This morning, after the coffee and the search for food in the refrigerator that isn't there, I finally get up off of the couch. I grab my 20 journals that I've been writing for nearly 20 years and I read my story.

I hold one hand over my left eye and read. I read all day until I find a recent entry on a dream where a woman handed me a journal with the title 'Creating Forward.' I must have thought the dream was meaningless at the time, but at least I had a pinpoint of inner direction to write down this dream.

Creating Forward. This will be the title of my book.

This thought gets me off of the couch, for only the 2nd time today. After a quick restroom break which just makes my head and eye throb more, I get a cloth and tape it over my left eye. I retrieve a blank journal from deep within my nightstand and brush the dust away. I write on its cover 'Creating Forward.' I write on its first blank page my inner desires on how it can help people so they don't end up on the couch: *'Creating Forward' is to enlighten on being pulled forward from that full, mature, bountiful and abundant Being that wants so badly to exist. This is about getting there, hopefully without the pain than I've put myself through.*

I re-write some of my earliest journal entries. I start seeing my own story on paper. And then I fall asleep, pen in hand, cloth on eyeball.

I awake knowing that my suffering is just my resistance to the oak pulling on the acorn. What if that beautiful, abundant Sara is my oak tree? What if her existence is pulling me forth? Is she my future, my ending? It's just that the pain on the surface reflects the pain in my soul and it overwhelms my ability to function. I want others to take care of me today.

I call my friend for a Reiki treatment and sluggishly take a shower. I'm out the door in my black yoga pants, the ones that never get used anymore, and a heavy black tunic. Since I didn't feel like making myself coffee, I turn off the desolate parkway into a gas station parking lot filled with trucks hauling boats. I park and walk my way through the wall-to-wall Ford F150s only to come upon the vehicle parked front and center. Paul's vehicle. I know it. I recognize the purple hanging football from the rearview mirror, that ornament that I have sat behind again and again.

I start to turn and run. But, it's too late. I see him through the window. I see him. I see his wife. I see him smiling. He's drinking my coffee, my caffeine; he's stealing my laughter and my alertness. He's' smiling. How can he possibly smile when he is apart from me? How can he go on? He's paying no penitence for his lies, for the dagger he pushed through my heart.

I turn and attempt to be invisible edging through the trucks, but everything about me is noticeable. My eye looks like someone has taken a baseball bat swing to it. The nerves palpitate like my heart. The pain wins and I bend over holding my left eye with both hands. My heart stops. I practically crawl to my car and then drive it across the street to park in a Wendy's parking lot as I don't know if I can go any further on this day in which I'm supposed to have someone else take care of me. The coffee was taken by someone whom I thought loved me.

It's a loss. The day is a loss. Paul stole my smile and how dare he take my space in life. I want him to hurt. I think he should pay for these shingles that his weakness has created in my body. He should suffer!

The pain in my body is now too great to ignore. I can either drive the 3 miles back home to lie on the couch or I can drive the 3 miles to Bruce's home where he can comfort me with Reiki. I'll do anything to make this suffering end. Keeping my left eye closed, I drive to see Bruce.

After the shock on Bruce's face, hugs and tears I am deep into my pain on the Reiki table. I have no place else to go. Into the pain. I want Bruce to say the right words, to ease my discomfort and tell me that he sees me and Paul together one day.

Instead, the discomfort increases. The blood in my eye pounds at my nerves. I surrender, as there is nothing left that I can do. Suddenly, in my mind's eye, I am standing in the acting studio of my childhood. I see myself, my 5-year old self, standing in the corner amidst an early-life drama. I was cute - with dark brown, curly pony tails sticking straight out each side of my head and the straightest damn bangs imaginable.

I realize that I should follow this, as it must be a part of myself that I need to understand or to heal. I look closer and realize that my 5-year old self is crying. I was crying so damn hard in the corner of that drama studio. I did not want to act. Imagine that! How could that be? I love to act. I spent my childhood on stage after stage. I was Dorothy, Sacajawea, a princess and both Wendy and Peter Pan. I sang at church in *It's a Wonderful Life* and took parts in *Joseph and the Amazing Technicolor Dreamcoat* in my adult life. I can't imagine why I would have cried over acting.

I was shy! Shy! This is a surprise to me. I don't recall being shy; I don't remember being scared of just acting. But this 5-year-old does not want to act! I feel her feelings and look into her eyes and I see clearly that she is scared of being judged by those who watch her. She wants to go home to her dogs and to the love of her grandpa. Love. She was searching for love not judgment. She was searching for acknowledgement for who she truly was. She wants to play Chutes and Ladders with grandpa and cheat at the game, just to ensure he wins.

I couldn't stand the thought of Grandpa losing. I loved him

completely. He couldn't hurt; he could never hurt. I wouldn't let it happen. *Not allowing others to hurt. What is that? Control? Fear of your own pain?* That's how my love is and that's how I expect love to be. I'm so conflicted. I expect others to not want to hurt me just like I did not want to hurt Grandpa. Isn't that love?

And more importantly, I now know that I didn't want to be on stage! Yet, that is exactly how my life unfolded. I became a strong, independent, stage-actress until I began teaching in drama school myself. I loved the show and I loved showing the characters off! To this day, I love being in front of crowds, and especially speaking to a crowd. It's because my mom left me at drama school, even though I was crying. She left me so I would get over my shyness. She turned me around. So, I went on to spend my childhood, adolescent and teenage years always busy, always practicing, always working at the next performance. I put on makeup, high heels, pink-fluffy boas, western gear, my strong southern accent and my learned New York slang. People knew me, so I had to do everything right. I got straight A's, played sports, started the high school debate team, and became the Honor Society President and the Latin Club President. I let my boyfriend take the job of Student Council President. I didn't want to hurt him; so I gave him something. I definitely got over my shyness.

Or, did I? Lying deep within myself on this Reiki table, with Bruce guiding my energies higher, I now clearly see that this sweet, love-hungry 5-year old did not grow up. A personage grew up. A mirage developed to overshadow the weakness of the shy girl. That persona is now argumentative, exacerbating and sometimes destructive, oppressed, and depressed. The real me never grew up, never learned how to handle challenges, never understood that many others treat life and love as a game, merely a game. And every so often, when I feel that connection, the kind that makes my heart skip a few beats, the kind of purity that the 5-year old had with Grandpa, it is her that comes out, wanting love and intensity in love. She wants that true connection with that same love and trust that Grandpa gave.

That young child came to Earth to be the sensitive and to build her life, play her life from these talents. She does not know how to play because someone else took over. And now she is emerging. That's why I can't get my bearings. That's why I'm overcome with emotion and am distraught. The personage can't fight any longer by taking control and making happiness a game. The personage must give up control, must die.

Bruce's work helped my heart to feel lighter. But back home, on the couch it is the thoughts of seeing Paul today that overtake the peace that could be in my heart. A heavy weight, circling in my head and body exists yet I can't find where it starts. If I knew where it started, if I recognized the source, I could put it out. It just hangs here in pain, in desperation, in a disturbed space recalling that smile on Paul's face, drinking my coffee.

I attempt to put thoughts of hope into my mind, but the reality wins. My flesh feels it. It's eating my flesh, my body. It's tearing from my core out. It wants to be released. Why do I hold on to this fiend? Why do I feed this aching, hateful, fearful sadness? Why is it still hanging there? I could be happy. I want intensity. I want my true self. I want my intensity to be loved, adored, to be taken in with someone else's humanity.

I reach for my journals and find the one that contains the letter that I wrote to Hugh over 10 years ago. Hugh was my spiritual affair. He was the man, twenty years my senior, who had written his own book on the afterlife and later moved to New Orleans to begin a healing arts center. He was the man that God brought to me. The outcome of our relationship was the realization of my worst fears. I could not trust God. True love, a spiritual love, denied me.

I loved Hugh so deeply and wholly that each breath felt like a manifestation of that enrapture. We were drawn together the moment our eyes met. Our souls had met an eternity before and we were still playing to the same symphony. He was the part of my soul in which I was searching. His tender touch was the awareness that on some level our souls had a purpose together. I reached out to entwine with his soul. The intensity destroyed the old me, but the process took years. The suffering didn't have to go on for years, but I kept it there as a reminder that I'm alive and that I suffer from True Love, not American suburbia love. Nephertiti still sits by my bed.

Hugh,

I'm writing this letter because I need to explain exactly the way I feel. I feel deeply that I love you. When I see you I shake inside because the energy between us is so strong. I don't know what to do with it and I don't understand why a connection so strong and deep cannot be had on the physical realm. Isn't the physical realm important, too? Wouldn't a love relationship this deep stand the test of time? (I guess it does, since I'm writing about him 16 fucking years later). *When I think of spending a lifetime with you I see myself yearning deeply to be in your arms every day. I see myself always desiring to show you how much I love you. Is this a fantasy; am I in love with being in love? To me, you are my soul mate.*

It hurts so deeply that you say you love me and then run away. I know you are torn. You would feel guilty if you experienced the true wealth of our love. It hurts like hell that you won't allow us this blessing. You mean completion to me. I'm at true peace in your arms, because of a Truth that is beyond words. I refuse to live another lifetime without you. I want to share myself and my being with you. If you don't want to be with me or if you don't have it within yourself to make the necessary changes to be with me, then so be it. I will wish you well and hold much love for you forever, no matter how distant we are. If you do choose to be with me, I will be forever truly free and each moment with you will be a heavenly gift.

I love you,
Rebecca

He did not choose to be with me, and I did not wish him well. And now another Love. Paul. Story unfinished.

I find the pages in my journal where I got a message from Sara in my sleep: *Love unconditionally, from a distance, grow toward this feeling of success until you come together. Open all doors. Don't be motivated by fear. Be motivated through feeling successful, which only comes as a result of releasing the struggle. Shut thoughts out that don't reflect high vibrations. Do not resist your deepest desires and they will come to you. Invest in the relationship from a distance, from freedom by growing happiness. The outcome is a state of being, not a place.*

It's so cathartic to get out what's been pinned up inside. I write a few words in what one day will be my book: *Find peace wherever you are at. Align with trust. The outcome is about getting to a state of being; it is not a place, an award or an act. But, I wake up some days filled with Anguish and It must be placed to pen and paper. To awake with Anguish, I must be inviting Him to bed.*

Now I lay me down to sleep

I pray the Lord my soul to keep

If I shall die before I wake

I pray the Lord my soul to take

CHAPTER 6
Forwarding

Rebecca has been forwarding her emotions to her persona for a very long time. She doesn't see this yet. She has yet to realize that she is acting in a drama on a stage called Longing. This longing is apparent in her childhood. Her grandfather gave her energy through giving his love to her young soul. This energy felt like expansion; it felt like she was living in the place from which she had just come, spirit. Disconnected from this energy creates the longing, and it is this disconnect in which she built the stage of her life.

Although Rebecca can choose to feed her soul, she is now too deep in darkness. She doesn't even recall that she can get the energy from nature, the same love that she received from her grandfather. Her stage of life has been made so concrete by destitute longings, looking in the opposite direction for love, and by her societal reality, a space so unconsciously filled with fear that the people there have created prayers of fear, that she's ready to fall into the pain of millions. She wants to find out what happened and find that place within herself that needs healing. She wants to heal the past. Yet, she does not have the full picture of the complexity of the past. It is ingrained in all consciousness. Her persona tapped into the possibility of fear, with a tapping so gentle and an access wide open.

Rebecca would have quick healing if she ousted that persona

from herself, that persona that took over the life of the young soul and tapped into the human-created astral plane. Her young soul knew Rebecca's destiny. Her persona does not. Subconsciously, Rebecca is sleeping with demons, and it is in her desire to heal her past that she meets the demons of universal consciousness face-to-face.

CHAPTER 7
Seduction

My husband left me within weeks of my first site of Hugh. He was ready to go. I had become stale and Elizabeth had become interesting. For nearly two years, I cried more than I spoke. Prone, seeking freedom from time, my body and mind dissolved into gray as a void unfolded within. As rotting meat attracts flies, devoured in a frenzy to get rid of what is no longer purposeful, the void both engulfed and consumed me. Moment lay upon moment. In a sort of emersion of the moments I cracked.

Before the dissolution, love was real, beautiful and tangible. I deserved love. I had found the love of my life. But when Hugh later left, I was gone but conscious as tangled matter without direction or growth or sustenance. At war with myself, my mind grasped to understand and often sprang toward hate and sometimes vengeance. Somewhere deeper, inner shifts toward truth brought pain, but the source was unrecognizable. The truth of his love and the truth of rejection played out, conceived with every desperate need, but conceivable only after the collapse of my mental, emotional and social wars. The battles both killed me and re-birthed me. Nevertheless, I would never make this mistake with love again.

The walls around my bed draw closer; the ceiling is the roof to my cave. My babies need me, yet I can't find the strength to be a mother, just as I had lost the strength after Hugh.

My journals remind me of that anger turned into a multitude of illnesses. *How could God let this happen? Why isn't God about true love? Why won't He let me have the same love that I give others? Why does God allow my daughter to have so much pain?*

And now again, my anger swells. My thoughts turn over and over, one on top and devouring another. *Everything that I have believed in has let me down. Wait, Perhaps that was the moment that I let the darkness in. Perhaps I've been asking the wrong question all along. Perhaps in that I moment that I screamed at my guides and at my angels and at God in blame that I actually met Anguish.*

How could I have ever denied them? It was definitely an angel who saved me from death by a jack-knifed truck during college. Driving up an icy highway slope, near Lake Superior, and as the snow fell harder and faster, I prayed out loud to make it home safely. There was no turning back, as the rush hour traffic filed in on every side of my small, black Mazda 2-door. Vehicles were neck to neck with me as my wheels slid sideways in a center lane. It happened so quickly. I can barely explain. The truck to my right jack-knifed violently in my direction and I saw a hand. Although I didn't brake or step on the gas, my car was flung through the small gap between the cars to my left, without touching one of them. The snap of the semi took another semi-truck out with it and they slammed together in the exact spot where my car and body would have been.

It must have been spirit guides who set up an 'accidental' meeting at my sister's wedding. It was my sister's wedding that took me home my senior year of college. Each summer I had been working to set my life in Wisconsin. A long term career was edging nearer. Yet a stranger came along to change things. Sitting at the round table with eight place settings at my sister's wedding reception, the new groom's friend, after not finding his name at any other table, asked if he could edge in as person number nine. After an evening of small talk, that apparently got him confident in my talents, he offered me a job. A good-paying job. This meeting took me back to the swamps.

I recognized the future father of my children when I passed him on my first day of work. That evening I called everyone who mattered, "I found my future husband! I found the man who will father the soul of my son!" (The son I'd been waiting for since at least third grade.)

Once we had met and the stage was set, spirits sent from God had to be the reason that I met so many lonely and dying people who asked for my comfort. In the name of Higher Love, I held several of them as they died. By this time I was working in several types of spiritual healing-arts. I gave my time, my love and my soul to strangers. Some calls came in the middle of the night asking for help. I did so freely. Many of these strangers told me that my presence brought them peace and relieved their suffering. This gave me a reason for living. Powers outside of me had to make that happen. I didn't go looking for these people. They appeared and each chance to work with them filled me with Love.

So why would the spirits bring me Hugh when they knew he wouldn't choose me? They knew how much my heart would break. So when my heart did indeed break I chose the response:

"I hate you God! I hate you God! I hate you angels and spirit guides and helpers! Don't come here again. I don't ever want to see you again!
"Never, never come into my space!"

This screaming went on for days once I reached the not-so-well accepted "acceptance" stage of my grief. Leaning over the side of my bed or lying on the floor outside of my bathroom, with a deep feeling of desolation and an inability to heal myself, I unleashed at God and all of those who represent Him

With my lifelong adoration for the spirits, the angels, and spirit guides, these screams were disconnects from my nature. The acts were my ultimate betrayal. Like a devout Christian screaming "scum" to Jesus or a Buddhist throwing His statue into the abyss to null enlightenment, I broke the silence. No human could shatter my belief in higher beings, in God, in enlightenment. But I did. Who else could have guided me to love but God and then snatch it away? Who else could have been responsible for removing happiness from my life? Who would hold such a plan?

At that time I felt there was no one else to blame. I hadn't done anything other than love.

Voices from other worlds began appearing, especially past midnight. Angry voices intensified as I could not sleep with the thoughts of all the people who had hurt me coming into view: "If you wink at me again, asshole, I will eat you for dinner." "My mother needs to never speak to me again, that abusive witch."

One evening, the voices solidified around 1:00am. I awoke to saliva in my navel. Another morning I heard guns, civil war guns and tasted blood in my mouth. My body broke down and stopped letting me know that it needed food or water.

And now I know. It is Anguish that I must meet and release from his duty.

The pecan tree haunts, bending toward me, reaching its arms into the window, trying harder and harder to break through and take me. The darkness outside is exactly that, a giant cave of lying people. Shams, pretending to like one another while buying their sedans, preparing a meal for a dying lady, and kneeling on their doorsteps before church to show how much better they are, and don't they have the new shoes show it!

As my eyes drift off to sleep, jaguars approach, stalking me and my stomach feels like an old, wooden, creaking door that expelled dust and moths and ghosts into the cracks of my being.

He arrives. And the memory of the evening that I unleashed my pain on Hugh and his family pops into my head. He starts with a gentle stroke on my upper left cheek and then runs his fingers through my hair. So gentle. A caress of my scalp sends tingles in places that have been dead for far too long.

"Remember?" he says. "Just relax. You'll be fine with me."

And then, I fall deep into sleep.

And when I awake in the morning, I have saliva in my navel once again. I wonder if it is manna from heaven, as it was that long-ago day of my near-death experience. Maybe I'm finally determined to heal and I'm leaving my body at night. I shower and dress to spend a day with my beautiful children and without being a depressive, lonely woman.

And the evenings grow. Each night the pecan tree dawns a new stature, one that reminds me of the dark, bent over, lonely skeleton that I had become. Each night this elusive man appears deeper and deeper into the breaks of silence in my head. But tonight his voice reaches me.

"I will help you understand. I will ease your pain by taking you to from where this comes. I am never alone, and nor should you be, my love."

I dream of running through dark tunnels, through trellises covered with dying grapes, as I look over my shoulder to the past for the person who is after me. I run and run as the trellises seem eternal.

Suddenly a hand reaches into the tunnel. A large, ghostly white hand stretches from afar, only to reach me. He will be the one to retrieve me out of this endless tunnel of death vines.

I let him take me.

Stillness, or perhaps nothingness, takes over. Despair vanishes. I am with him. We are standing in a field of green covered by a light fog and a silent moment or two lapses outside the tunnel. The fog parts and we step inside a great abbey of thick stone. The floors are ice cold and the walls even colder. The hallway cracks of something just around the corner. A noise ruffles the air from a hollow space and it draws us in. Dense grumbles seem to come from humans disconnected from their own voices. The sound of wood scratching across stone breaks my haze. I sense turmoil ahead.

We approach a heavy curtain embroidered with earthen browns and greens, hanging to separate those who matter from those who service. Roasted meet and aromas of flatly boiled vegetables catch me. A clamoring of voices and dishes grows louder, as does the noise of wood upon stone. I step to the curtain and peer through its crack. A rather large man of gregarious manners sits at the end of a table. His overwhelming control of the table by his attitude and the snap of fingers to a servant makes it clear that he is host. As the spread of the table comes more into view, I take in the eager guests and their impartiality to the buffet of magnificent proportions.

Gashan and I stand here, scanning the feast of joy, wine of deliverance and cold smiles that mask many unspoken truths. Drab but outspoken attire adorn everyone. Collars are high and starched on the men and shoulders sit like cloud puffs atop the shoulders of several women. The enjoyment in their eyes come from being tokens of their society. This is their enjoyment at the banquet. The food cannot deliver such sustenance without sharing and showing it off in the proper company. The host owns abundance and willfully shows others how to best display it. The others oblige, most certainly because it increases their chances of having a piece of the abundance.

Beef is forked out plate to plate and potatoes spooned on top as if the source birthed an endless supply. Glasses clank and cutlery spanks the plates from the embodied indulgence of their masters.

The host, who guests refer to as 'My Lord', speaks of becoming a step-father and then of becoming a father himself someday. His last wife, the winch, never bore him children. He continues on with tales of his abundant life now coming together with the Montague fortune. He and the lady to his left will be married in two days.

The cooked swine in the center of the table beholds an apple between its teeth and the gentlemanly old fellow at its back side, who shakes like a skeleton hanging in a biology lab, swiftly digs in without waiting for the servant. His patience has run thin. But, with the last cut of his knife the wine takes over. He brazenly tries slicing into a shallow piece of meat and his arm slips forward, propelling the knife forward and down into the lap of a beautiful young lady. The knife takes out a water glass while swine juice tears across the girl's face and gown. The adults laugh at the old man's clumsiness, but the handsome boy to the girl's right politely offers a napkin and calls a servant to help her with her attire.

Gashan tugs at my hand and pulls me up the stairs to follow the young lady. The servant had rushed her away quickly. Gashan pulls harder to get me to keep up. The trestle of her tea-green gown hugs the stone floor as she makes her way around each spiral and then down the hall of stone that upholds door after door of solid dark wood, closed to the spectators who want to do more than wonder what is kept within the walls.

The old, plump woman servant opens a small door at the end of the hall and swiftly leads the beauty through its opening. The door shuts and I am left wondering why Gashan has brought me here and why we should be so curious of this young lady.

Clanking of the dinnerware is no longer audible. Stone provides a solid barrier from the pretentious noises downstairs. I think of how it sounded like a brothel from inside that large, heavy room. Each individual digging into whatever is offered, hording the respective portion which was too large for a body to adequately digest, feels like a heavy inertia, darkness spiraling downward. Gorging, while pretending not to, was the theme of the night, not sharing.

Gashan stops a few doors before the lady's door and motions with a finger to his lip in an act of silence. His finger is so long and pale, but seductive. He slowly moves that finger to tenderly caress his lip and the tip of his nose before sliding the digit down, enticing me as he uncovers this sanctimonious portion of his face. I notice his deep and dark eyes and I peer into their depths, seeing that he holds much knowledge and many secrets. His intense look shows a deep knowledge that spans centuries.

With this understanding, I finally notice his clothes. He wears a heavy black cloak that folds at the wrists and hangs to the floor. His hat is double-rimmed, in the shape of a Bundt cake perched upon a rigid disc. But his feet, his feet are bare.

Gashan motions that I move closer to the door behind him.

Giggling is coming from behind the closed slab of wood. First, a girl asks for a hug and then a boy solicits the need to know if his gesture was enough. He giggles. Gashan asks me to step even closer and the sounds become clearer.

"Sit near me, dear brother. I love our time together."

"Yes. I don't want you to be sad. But Miss Agathe will soon notice that I have left my room," a young male voice responds.

"Don't you wish that we hadn't gone to Aunt Adrienne's that weekend? Her dinners were always meek. We didn't have to stay for that last one. If I had just made her call the horses sooner, we could have said goodbye to Papa. He hadn't died long before we arrived and I know he was alive on Saturday because I heard mother talking about it," the young female voice explains.

"Don't say that Anna. I don't want to remember it and you just make me sad."

They are speaking French; yet, I understand them fully.

Rustling overwhelms their words and I can no longer make out what they are saying within those walls. The rustling transports my mind home to my neighbor's horse stable. The stretching of that leather belt as she tightens it for my ride is what I was hearing. What am I hearing in the stone walls exactly? Stretching leather, wood screeching against stone and then moaning?

The return of the lady in green startles me. Gashan doesn't budge. The girl is cloaked in a cotton shawl to mask the stains beneath. She is in a rush to return to dinner, thanking the old lady politely but madly wanting to get rid of her. "Mr. Brady mustn't leave before I can properly bid him well. Please forgive me. I must run."

Everything falls silent behind the door until the old lady passes into the stairwell, noticeably descending as each garish brush of her cotton garments against the stone and wood mark her hurried, heavy stature.

Yes. It was stretching leather that I was hearing. I recognized it, rubbing against itself, pulling at the wood by the weight of those giggling children inside.

"Dawson, I can't live without you! I like your skin next to mine. I love the way you hold me and the feeling of your breath against my face. Without it, I would anguish in the loneliness that mother has placed us in."

"I am concerned about for our fate, sister."

"I feel the same, Dawson. It is not safe here. I am only safe in your arms, but this safety shall lead us to our fate."

"Precisely, Anna. We will be separated if someone finds us. I want you to try to be happy in this new home in England. I am beginning to like it. We must be careful," says the young boy.

"Mother left my nurse behind in France, but brought Miss Agathe for you. If my fate is left up to Mother, I will be married to a squire and will continue to be a prisoner. This abbey is filled with lies that Mother and the Lord are keeping and I have no way to escape this darkness. Your arms must forever be my fate, holding me in the safety of your steadfastness. You are strong, dear brother and your sureness will lead us out of these walls."

The talking ceases. Gashan's eyes are hollow as to not give me his interpretation of the event I just witnessed. He just allows me to digest it.

"She is scared, Gashan. She doesn't feel loved and is holding onto her brother in an attempt to feel safe. Otherwise she is lonely. She does not realize that she is taking from her brother, to weaken him and control him. She is unaware, Gashan. Perhaps the death of her father started this insecurity."

Gashan doesn't respond in voice, in gesture or with his eyes. He lets me decide.

Then slowly the block draws back without even a hint of light getting through to the hallway. The boy's eyes glisten through the darkness within the crack. He cautiously sticks his head out to peer in each direction and then runs toward the stairs. Just as sneakily, the door shuts itself.

As we turn to make our exit, the plump servant reappears in the passage and startles me. She turns into the door which stood between me and Gashan. "Come on Anna, get back out of bed and say your prayer before sleep. I know you haven't said it yet. If you don't pray, you could end up like your father. And worse, you won't be accepted by the Lord."

The stretching leather is much less than before. And this time, the stretching creeks of the leather straps are slow to unleash.

"Now I lay me down to sleep. I pray the Lord my soul to keep. If I shall die before I wake, I pray the Lord my soul to take."

CHAPTER 8
The Walk

A ringing phone nudges me awake. Grape vines, kinked and browned with decay, shroud my view as I emerge from sleep. My heavy head, full of doubt and angst, is barely supported by this flat pillow. I've been too dead to change the sheets. When will I again dream of butterflies, a buffet or my children's' smiles to awake happy?

I reach for the phone that I cannot find and the rings stop.

I roll back over, face in pillow. I pause in recognition of the space from which my mind just lapsed. That young, praying girl was so desperate for love. I still feel her, as I am not yet fully awake. I feel pity. She is absent of a family filled with love. Her parents don't care to her tender emotions, to her need for love. She wants recognition of the internal. She seeks peace but gets no direction. Appearances are more important to her parents, more important than the pain harbored inside their daughter.

I have dreamt of this girl before. Anna, the neglected and insecure girl who searches for love in desperate places. She has no ground on which to walk, no love line to direct her. The gruff noises and meaty smells of that stone abbey are in my bed.

Why is she back? Why did I recall her so clearly in sleep? Years ago I felt that Anna was a dream creation of my inner child longing for Hugh. She needed love and recognition, as did I. Love and understanding was not poured on me during those sensitive puberty years, so I searched for it in boys. I allowed myself to be intimate well before I was ready. If a child feels neglected or abused, especially while hormones are racing, neglect and abuse are always easily found. The inner will is broken.

The throbbing nerves have calmed to a mellow pulse. Although at times, lightning strikes across my skull, tearing me to a beaten down child. I get up as the phone again rings.

It is Dora. "Rebecca, there is a firewalk happening just two hours from your home this weekend!"

"How can I possibly firewalk now Dora? I barely have the energy to get out of bed. My eyeball throbs and I don't want to drive because the sun makes the pain worse."

"Excuses Rebecca, excuses! Get someone to drive you because I want to see the old firewalking Rebecca again!"

A couple of hours of writing about Anna and what I would say to Anna to make her wake-up about her desperation leads into a conversation with myself. I begin to realize that Hugh and Paul are my desperate longings. I'm looking outside of myself to find love. The vessel inside of me is empty. My outward reaching has broken my will.

I decide to use what little will that I have left to go to that firewalk. I call my dear friend James and ask him to drive me. I tell him that this is my effort to allow my soul to expand instead of contract. I tell him that it may seem like an extreme method of burning your inhibitions and fears away, but it works, so I hope he tries walking the coals himself.

James the Leo agrees as he is all fire and will be the center of the party.

I am more relaxed by the weekend. I've been meditating on how it felt to firewalk, in an attempt to bring more of my spirit into my body. I connected to the empowered me that held only excitement for that fire and never fear. I connected to the feelings that once propelled me across that fire. A little spark within my heart remembers, but my mind does not. The doorbell breaks my meditation and James and I are off to the unknown.

We reach the gravel road that will take us nearly 5 miles and dump us off at the celebration. Something does not feel right. There are abandoned cars along the way and one is covered by a confederate flag. My firewalks of the past were in the city, with people of different beliefs and styles. Every vehicle along the way now looks the same, impoverished and ready for a fight.

As we near the tents ahead, three men spot us from inside their parked truck. We get the evil eye and then I realize that this is going to be an all-white gathering, and one in which James, this big, dark hunk of a southern-Baptist preacher, could get shot. James also realizes this and offers to drop me off and return to pick me up in 5-hours. I usually would refuse this offer but I have to walk this fire. I have to regain my will.

After watching James' truck pick up dust, I turn and take in a waft of marijuana smoke, half-naked white bodies lying across a ground speckled with American Bluehearts, and the three men emerging from the truck looking like they might have just stored their hoods on a hook. I realize that I've just been dropped off at a Get-Back-to-Nature Not-so-Spiritual-Whitefest!

I am able to keep somewhat invisible during the events leading up to the firewalk, including being cloaked from the five men building the fire. I don't give my real name to anyone and just sit in an abandoned chair within the shade and watch the activities.

It is getting dark and heavy trees sway in front of the full moon as the fire is about burned down to its embers.

The firewalking leader emerges from a tent. It's obvious, as her face is filled with pride and she gives no attention to anyone. She expects everyone to follow her. And follow they do, but not across the fire.

I leave my chair to be one of her followers, slowly meandering toward the fire. I remain hidden in the back as to keep all attention from myself. If I were leading this walk, I would have connected with people from the heart. I would have created a drumming circle hours ago to increase the vibration and to get people into their spirits. There has been none of this here. If these swampers realize my disgust for their leadership, they might hang me. So, I stay hidden.

She begins her preparatory speech. "Your safety is my priority and this is why the walk is only 12 feet long instead of the customary 18 feet. There is plenty of ice in the cooler if you were to get a blister, and I promise you if you do indeed get a blister, it will be small. I usually don't hear complaints about blisters. Blisters are not that common."

Blisters….blisters..blisters…blah blah blah blah. Not a single word of motivation or connection comes out of this woman's mouth. Instead of igniting the soul of the group she just ignited the fear of getting burned. She just manifested blisters!

The group motivation is lacking. There is no group spirit, only a fissure in the group. An hour of no activity ticks by, as the embers are being spent. She just spent this last hour trying to remove her words and prove that no one would get burned. But, she already unleashed fear and pain and the crowd recognized it in themselves. She cannot now remove it from them. I watched as people began visibly swimming in their minds amongst their fears.

I have never stood back from a fire; I always walked immediately. And now the disappointment of the day is more than clear. The fire will soon be out and I'll get burned if I take the chance.

The leader leaps into the fire, exits the walk and I see red-hot embers glued to her foot. She still implores the crowd to step-in and step-up. A few do. I watch. They are getting burnt, and they aren't walking, they are running! It's like a tip-toe spring through the tulips so you don't crush your mother's back. And there they go, toe-toe-LEAP out of the garden that's burning my toes!

I am scared and disheartened. This is firewalking! I love

firewalking and it heals me. I can't turn away from this fire. Then, my chance appears. Everyone turns from the fire and a void is present between myself and that fire. This is my chance to show them how it is done. I'm full of uncertainty yet I walk up anyways. I take a deep breath. *I'm going to do whatever it takes to WALK across this damn fire!* I wipe all of the leader's words from my mind. I start over. It is time to ascend suffering. The presence in my heart, the desire that is pulling me forward at this time in my life is my love for Paul. His actions are of no concern. Love is present in my heart for him. I feel so much joy just feeling my love for him. I release the disappointments from my mind. I love him! I smile a little precocious smile of epiphany. I hold Paul in my heart and smile. I feel the pure, innocent love that he once had for me. There is no such thing as time, so he still loves me. My smile grows larger. But another epiphany enters my consciousness. His love for me is irrelevant. It's my love that matters. It is this love that pulls me into Being who I am meant to be, and I am meant to walk this fire! So, I walk with this powerful love and I walk slowly, deliberately, without pain and without any burns.

I exit the walk in pure relief and realize all pain is gone from my eyeball and head. I feel love! I turn back around and slowly walk these burning embers again. I love him, I love him! That's a beautiful thing! I walk a 3rd time and now get a little egoish thought that I hope the leader is watching. And one last time, with a stranger brave enough to follow behind, I walk very, very slowly, feeling the intense heat beneath my feet and in-between my toes. I step off of the walk unharmed and notice what hadn't been in my line of sight before.

There is a hut outlined by the light of the night sky and there is a man, a brilliant shaped man adorning it. He removes his cloak to bare his skin, his sculpted body and his loins. I watch him bend down to his knees, kiss the earth and then upwardly stretch, arms raising outward and then high to the sky. He is long, lean and buff, apparent by his silhouette lining the light emitted from inside the hut. And there is a dagger on the ground, a lunar shadow cast by his manhood.

I return to the firewalkers, pretending he is not there.

I am so relieved and all it took was to hold love in my heart. In this case, it is my love for Paul. In that love, there are no disappointments. And in this love, I walk fire.

I make my way through the brush to get to the drumming circle, knowing that soon James will arrive to take me home. I'm concerned about him traversing that dark gravel road alone. So I keep my ears open wide to hear his tires make their way down the path.

My hands begin pounding the drum and soon the drum is beating to the rhythm of my heart. I know that I just accepted my true desire, to love. Perhaps it is love for Paul. Perhaps it is love for my purpose. I stop resisting. The leader's talk was resistance and it is in resistance that we 'get burned'.

James is very late and I think he may have decided to not return at night. I try over and over again to reach him on his cell phone but there is no service out here. I find a young couple willing to give up one of their tents. I spend some time gathering blankets and a pillow. I peak my head out of the tent and there is James! James is being handed a drum at the drumming circle and the three men from the truck are glaring at him. I run to him, greet him, hug him, and damn it warn him through a whisper that he should not take that drum.

There are rules with this drumming circle. There is a leader. Everyone follows the leader. The leader plays the loudest. The leader makes the rhythm. And most definitely, we were not to start our own rhythms! My drum had been rising and falling with the leader's beat for more than an hour before James arrived.

James takes the drum from the nice lady against my advice. "Have you ever played before?" she asks him. His answer is a firm "No."

Within one minute he has a rhythm, a damn good rhythm; it beats to my heart. Within two minutes he is performing the first sacred sin of the ceremony, playing much louder than the boss. Within five minutes, he has his own rhythm, a rhythm much better than anything we have heard thus far. A magnificent cadence pulses through everyone. His music tells a story in emboldened magnitude, sweeping through our perceptions of all that is possible. His music uplifts in glory and there is dancing and chanting and hugging. James' beat leads to love between us all. Love, except for the three men who have been gravely peering at James the entire hour.

James appears to be a professional drummer and looks like the coolest, polished, most confident man alive. Yet, this is the James who fears the loss of love; the James who never accepts a solid relationship that he deserves. I wonder if he holds a belief deep inside that he is not worthy of his own worth.

James puts down the rhythm to his soul, calmly rises from the wooden stump and five women gather around him like body guards, swiftly walking him to his truck. The spirit of the place dies abruptly with his departure.

James has never played a drum before, but apparently his soul has. His rhythm came from the depths of his Being that is trying to be born. This is the real James; this is his oak tree in a moment of explicit drawing force on the acorn. Not only was this creative spirit drawing James forth, but all of us present. We are to be more than we accept.

After the quick reflection on my friend, I grab the couple whose tent I would have borrowed and have them walk with me side-by-side to the car holding the black man.

I pick my journal up from the nightstand, the journal that holds my darkness and love. I must get some feelings into words, this inner restlessness into words, because I must feel free enough to go back to work tomorrow against the will of my body and soul.

Just one night with that chiseled man would be awesome. I don't even know if he is attractive. *Maybe it was the moonlight that drove my attraction. Who is he?*

I laid down my ego Saturday. Paul betrayed my love so obtrusively; yet, I allowed my heart's love for him to slowly guide me across that fire. Love lifted me to an energetic place where I remembered that I am one with everything, including Paul. If I am one with the fire, I am the fire and the fire can't hurt me. If I am one with Love, I am Love and love cannot hurt me. It is best to not focus on the doings of others.

Another week at work. Daily routines of anxiousness at my desk and mulling over the proper writing of an e-mail until my eyeball stings. I'm still waking up well before the sun rises. No need to set an alarm clock. My mind and body are too restless wondering how I will get out of this meaningless job and wondering if Paul is back in Atlanta for eternity.

I try my best to flow with life. I try to keep the love that took me across the fire in my heart and mind. I must repeat and repeat the feeling until I know nothing else. I go on to shower, go to work, and repeat.

I sleep better for a few nights.

The light above my office desk is too potent for my damaged cornea, so I go to the bathroom and cry. I close the door to the stall and the toilet lid and sit hoping no one will enter and hear me. I have three hours left of work, but no energy to finish. The confusion is returning but from where I am not sure.

What if? Why? How could he? Why would he? I still love him. This place is tyrannical; this work numbs my soul. And the thoughts go up, cresting as I drive my emotions into them. The emotions then break my gut as I perceive all of the pain that has been done to me and will be done to me and most especially the self-inflicted pain because maybe I was just simply wrong. Maybe I'm so weak that I've messed this all up. I should have listened to him, loved him and not run away.

I make it home for another lonely night. My mind wonders from fear to explanation and back to fear as my hand wanders across the blank pages of my journal. I grab my pen because something sinister needs release.

My reality is painful, yet I don't tell Paul. I cry almost daily, if only for a minute. Yet, I don't tell anyone of these feelings. My stomach hurts constantly because my love was ripped apart right here in the depth of my being where I stored everything. Yet, I don't ask Paul if he has this same feeling. My ego won't let me ask. Yet, my ego doesn't make me happy.

Do I raise my sword? Do I fight this; fight this relationship that takes advantage of my kindness?

Sweating more in this dark cave, but only drops of water do I hear,
The dark side of my soul rests here.
I find fear here, no it found me.
I created it, then allowed it to create me.

I recall that lean and proud naked man at the firewalk. Light crept from the small space between his angled legs. Candles within his temple illuminated beads of sweat that glistened like stars in the night. He stretched his body toward mine. He adorned his penis and his lean, silky chest by extending them toward the moonlight as if to reach only me.

"Oh my God, Gashan!"

CHAPTER 9
Return to Darkness

It has been three months and still no contact with Paul, only the daily swipe of the scalpel across my eye and the random migraine. I plan to get away to the mountains, to my favorite spot on earth, red rocks within the Rocky Mountains. But I first must complete a work project and attend a mandatory team-building as new people are entering our project.

Dressing for the morning I notice that I'm choosing the tightest pants I can find, not corporate pants, but white French-styled pants with zippers at the ankles. I choose my sapphire-ruffled blouse and high heels. I've never worn high heels to work. And then I know. My subconscious is picking up on something that is not fully in my awareness. I am dressing for Paul. He is in town.

I start to shake as I make my way down the stairs and out to my car. I'm not thinking clearly. This would be the worst thing that could happen right now. I do not want to see the man who tore my heart wide-open. Yet, the way I am dressed says that I'm expecting to see him.

And there he is. Standing at the entrance to the meeting room, just waiting to see me. "Hi Rebecca."

I give him the middle finger. My anger is exploding. I have to sit through a 3 hour team-building carrying the face of disgust while he smiles and cracks jokes at the team.

After work, I skip-out on my son's baseball game and head straight home, straight to bed. I don't even start packing for my vacation.

My mind won't stop. All the 'whys?' *He used to tell me how much he missed me, even after being gone for one day. He couldn't say that today? He couldn't say that he misses me? That weak fucking loser could only say 'hi'?*

I fall asleep longing for love again, for human touch. "Why, why, why?"

I awake at 1:00am with a bladder needing relief of the wine. This nightly ritual leaves me begging to fall back to sleep. This night, I pray as I walk back to the bedroom. Nothing else has worked.

The voice in my head separates from me and takes a life of its own. It is so powerful that I can't just let it go; I can't just let it sleep.

The reminder of his love swells in disbelief around me. I stop praying and fall to the floor. I throw my fists into the air and scream, "How could you! You didn't love me! Love does not pretend to protect and pretend to be committed to just turn your back when it's convenient!"

A twig of the pecan tree scratches my window in a sharp, aching screech. Yet, there is no wind outside. I get off of the floor to investigate but only fall into bed. The bed is hot to the touch, as if I had never left it. My heartache is real. The air is still but someone is listening.

"Your feelings never mattered to Paul. Allow me to care."

My eyes fall closed and his hand softly caresses my shoulder, coursing in a subtle melody down my arm. The tingles let me drift deep into my body, so deep that there is no pain. I let go. Drifting within myself I am gently pulled through nothingness, through painless awareness.

Peace. I awake in a garden of pines swaying in the breeze. The sun is shining and I feel alive. I realize death lies back in my bed.

Gashan holds my hand. He moves my arm forward, pointing toward the center of a tall garden. The clearing is rectangular and is filled with tables draped by sea green linens. Motioning at the statues who call themselves humans, he urges me go amongst them and observe from the back of the garden. I slowly make my way through starched bodies and tall chairs, glimpsing back at each stern posture, dress and movement of this pale-faced party.

Gashan joins me at a table empty of guests but filled with every fixture needed to embellish high society. Silver, in the forms of three forks of varying sizes, a spoon large enough to feed a cow and extra spoons and a multitude of knives lie on top of brown linen napkins. They are obstacles to me; this décor is for others. There is barely space for my elbows to rest on the table.

The crystal bowl centerpiece sparkles with inlaid diamonds and holds resting lilies, lavender, green leaves and figs atop a pond of sparkling water. What I imagined to be sea green linens are actually silks, as are the scarves that hang over the back of each chair. Silver and silk were not imagined for my wedding. Centerpieces never crossed my mind. It was the celebration of love with family that kept my attention, although the presence of my son held the attention of others. Fine dining was not proper for a woman's wedding that took place after the child.

A flutist plays behind us and guests converse before us, in haughty English. Everyone is enjoying a celebration of their place in society. Nearly a hundred women are here eliciting their place in life. Drab-colored, frock dresses lift their buttocks. The boost in dress makes them seem almost colorful, both the dresses and the women. Their eye movement and gestures are not colorful but suspicious. A hand covering the mouth for only those near to hear says, "My words denigrate the other guests because I must find a way to feel good about myself when this dress is simply not enough."

I am not impressed.

Children play quietly but are loathed when they have to be seated. The Lord calls for attention. Guests take their seats, which are now hidden by the monstrous garments protruding off their backs. "Quiets' are called out with firm voices and harsher looks. Women continue to point and whisper in a sort of confusion over today's ceremony.

I scan the garden and see the new bride approach. The bride and groom gently smile at each other, but not to the crowd. Their dignity needs to be preserved. Everyone is here in the couples' honor. At least the smile to one-another seems real, joyful and trusting. They seem to be truly happy together. The gentle love that is shared between their eyes reminds me how I loved Paul, and how I loved the others.

A gloomy boy, of about 14, walks to the couples' side. He stares at the ground as they are ushered under a grove of trees. He nervously swings his thin leg right and left. His tan knickers rub together. The woman's hand on his shoulder is to calm him down. I now recognize them, at least I recognize 'The Lord.'

"Gashan, is that Anna's brother?"

"Possibly, but this boy isn't giggling."

"Is Anna also the same age as when I first saw her a decade ago?" I ask Gashan.

"Of course. Rebecca, do you think they would change on your time? Do you believe this moment changed? It is forever etched in the Earth's web."

"But, I have changed. I no longer love Hugh and I have no reason to see Anna again and her desperations"

"Really? Then how does this place make you feel? I heard your thoughts and I saw the gloom on your face as you eyed every person here. How does it make you feel, Rebecca?"

"It's just a celebration of a marriage. The garden is beautiful."

"Then why was your attention on the silver and the silk? Why do you hate these women?"

"I don't hate these women; I just don't agree with their false road of supposed happiness."

"If you haven't finished digesting this moment, Rebecca, it will always stay inside of you. You can return to it at any time to acknowledge and relinquish it, or you can choose to just let it play out in your subconscious forever."

"What on earth do you mean? I don't know these people! This is not my space," I spatter back.

"It is your space, Rebecca. Notice your feelings so you may heal them. Were you not just disturbed by the centerpiece and the silk and the silver? Whom does it remind you of?"

"I know you want me to say my mother, but I forgave her long ago."

"The disgust on your face says there is something you have not forgiven. If you had truly forgiven, then your heart would not react in such a negative way. Your mother chased fine furniture more than she chased your fine heart. Your faint heart searched for love, but it found Hugh. Hugh feared loving you because he could lose his possessions. Now, Paul is the same. They are your mother. You may think you have forgiven your mother, but your heart keeps bringing her into your life over and over again."

"How can you say these things?"

"Don't you wish to feel better, Rebecca? If you wanted to heal yourself and be happy you would be looking for Anna right now, not noticing the silver and the dresses and the talk. Every time you put your attention on these things, the universe organizes what you believe into your reality. Choose to heal yourself, Rebecca. I brought you here to heal this moment in time."

I scan the yard for the plump servant or the young lady in green. Oh, how I hope that Anna's pain has subsided. I don't know how to recognize her. "Where is Anna?"

"She's not here in the garden, Rebecca."

"She must be angry. Her father is dead and now her mother is making her new husband the priority. And on top of all of that, her servant put the fear of hell into her with that prayer of possibly not waking up from sleep. She's probably crying somewhere, locked away in fear."

Gashan turns, asking me to make a way of my own behind the

grove of trees. I slowly move forward and notice that I'm still wearing my pajamas.

A man they call Louis heaves a large box onto a table while the newlyweds pose for the anxious man. "That's a daguerreotype, Gashan"

"What else would it be?"

"Well, how do I know that? I've never seen one."

I weed through this past land and people to find that troubled girl who I'd love to hug, to just let her know that everything will be ok.

I walk past red chrysanthemums that are opened to the sun in a glorious togetherness, expressing the beauty of the day. I step on some garments and smell heinous perfumes. There are whispers in the air about the Lady. "She remarried so quickly. Her husband was just buried in the winter and I heard he was poisoned. Her relatives are not here. They would be here if she were an innocent woman."

It is Tuesday and everyone who could be anyone in this city must be here. At least the gentry are here. Staunch fedoras make the occupiers look like statues who breathe only coldness off their thick skins. The Lady of the evening wears a dress of ivory, with smoky-colored jewels embroidered in it. The jewels float down the gown as wisps of feathers. Her dark, squared hat matches the jewels in color but not in style. Her hands remain cupped in those of her husband.

I step closer to scan the faces of the guests, hoping to find Anna, but to no avail. The young lady from the long-ago dinner feast wears again a green gown, but this one smokes of emerald. It sits high on her shoulders and smelters down each arm to form solid at the wrists. Nothing is exposed except the pale, dainty face donning a tender smile of hope.

I step back from them to think how this relationship could be more important than Anna's wellness. Others are closing in with looks of awe at the photographer. A lean, smiling man, of about 20, approaches.

The lord beams with pride as he releases his hands from his

wife. Motioning to the young lady in green, he welcomes the young gentleman by his side. "My dear niece you remember Aaron. Aaron is making a fortune, my dear, as a railway and tool manufacturer. He sells equipment to places as far away as Russia. His father and I have a deep history. Since they will be staying here for the remainder of the season, he will be able to attend the grand balls. I will leave the two of you to talk this as I might talk my own business with Aaron's father. Exports out of Ireland are increasing every day!"

"Yes, my Lordship. Your niece and I will find much to attend to at your bequest."

"So be it. I will be on my way," the newlywed responds. And the photo-taking moment is over.

This young beauty's gown seems to be made of the finest silks and lace. It's the most vibrant emerald green I've seen except for the gem itself. The color drowns the green grass in a blanket formed in a gentle whirl. This girl is looking for love. She is shy, peering down, as not to catch Aaron's eye too often. Her tender face is a cool white, contrasting the dark locks surrounding it.

It does not take long before several of the most garish women approach her, including Anna's mother. They talk of what a fine lady Josephine is and how she has studied music since she was three. This conversation is obviously intended for Aaron, who stands gazing in wonder at Josephine. Anna's mother quickly becomes the leader of the conversation. She hackles on about how Josephine has the finest dowry from her late father and that her mother's family is known for bearing large families. Her mother owns an Indian silk company and has much to offer every time she comes home. The upcoming ball will be the perfect time to display the newest gown that Josephine designed herself. No other lady at the ball will look like Josephine. She will stand out and will have the eyes of everyone. Many young men have called to the abbey for Josephine's hand. But the right man will have as much to offer as Josephine.

"So, this is it. Love based on money, on items of luxury. She should want him because of his wealth and he should love her because of her wealth and ability to bear a large family." I say to Gashan but there is no Gashan here to respond.

As the new Lady Kelly finally turns to greet more guests and partake of the cakes and tea, Dawson sullenly appears by her side.

"Dawson, at least learn to look happy. These are my guests and they came here to celebrate, not become suspicious of our standing and fortune in town. If you continue to frown, you must go inside."

"I expected to see some of my cousins today, mother. I expected some family of our own, and some mix of French and English."

"Nevermind. This is your family."

"But Anna never came out to the garden. She returned to her room after the ceremony and she won't talk."

"I never expected her to act any other way. It is soon time for dinner and she has no choice but to be at the table with her new family. Now off to get Anna!"

Smiles grow large on the faces of the crowd around Josephine. Aaron bows with a large grin, possibly due to an acceptance of the invitation to the ball.

The ladies swarm Josephine and talk is off of the newlyweds and onto a possible new courtship.

"Dinner is served," is belted from the back entrance to the abbey. This shocks me since there was just quite an extravaganza in the garden.

As the women grab their parasols and the men their hats, guests politely and cautiously make their way into the abbey, behind Dawson who is running.

Emptiness hits me. Where is Gashan? Where could he have gone? Guests filter out of the garden, leaving only servants to tend to dirty plates and tea cups.

I grow fearful. Gashan is nowhere to be seen. I run behind the line of trees in hopes that he had been watching from afar, but no Gashan. I run to the stone walkway around the abbey and make my way around the whole of the great structure.

"Gashan? Gashan!" I scream.

I make my way into the abbey, up the spiral staircase and into the servants' chambers, where I had first heard Anna. Servants are steadily moving in and out of their rooms with varying attire, but no sign of Gashan. I run back down to the great room where an orchestra is playing and people are anxiously awaiting the food. I scan each table, each corner of the room and then run inside the kitchen where still there is no evidence of Gashan.

How could I have separated from him? Why did I get so lost? How will I get back home if Gashan isn't with me? I'm forgetting where home is.

As I leave the great hall, I brush aside a tearful Anna and a consoling Dawson who is leading his loving sister to their table of strangers. I stop before exiting the abbey just to see the presence of the two siblings at their mother's wedding celebration. The heavy, wooden tables are occupied by the Lord and Lady's distinguished guests, the niece and Aaron by his parents, and others who don't fit into Anna's family.

Anna and Dawson sit near but are not attached to the distinguished table. They apparently belong separate to the centerpiece and their feelings have no place for this day. Dawson continues to hold his sister in his right arm as the others seated at their table laugh amongst themselves, neglecting to notice the atmosphere surrounding the two young, disturbed children.

It is darker outside, but is getting clearer that I may not find Gashan. I run by the left side of the stark nymph fountain and then to the farthest end of the garden. I panic and have to make one more yell with all of my might.

"Gashan!"

A servant startles. He drops a tea cup onto a silk covering at the sound of my word. He anxiously grabs the tea cup back into his hand and slowly turns around, facing me directly. He has an awkward look on his face as if he may have just seen a ghost. He peers into my being and then looks around in doubt. His eyes move with his thoughts that tell him "it was nothing". Once he convinces himself that he heard nothing, he quickly grabs every remaining trinket on the table and dashes away.

He heard me. I have become too close to this place, too attached. Where is home?

I have no place to go but to Anna. I return to her table and overhear her whispers. "Why Dawson? How could God let this happen? I have always been so good and Daddy was so good to us. How could God take daddy and leave us with no one who cares? We've been so good."

"Please don't Anna. I will hold you again soon after dinner. Mom will get mad if she sees us sad. I will hold you this evening."

"Mom doesn't care about our feelings. She only cares about what these people think of her."

Wow, I've uttered those same words so many times in my own life.

"They can never separate us, Dawson. I would die without you. You are my love, my brother, my closest friend. They don't care. They are feasting and celebrating after daddy just died."

"Yes, Anna. But, this was true in France as well. Mother and father always celebrated with feasts, even after terrible events."

"You are the only love that I have. I can't lose you."

And again, words that I've uttered so many times in my own life.

I fall to my knees and my eyes well with tears.

I awake with my bed drowned in tears. In this moment of awakening, I decide to get out of this pain, away from my life by the cane river and out of the corporate world. I must not believe that Paul is my only love. I cannot lose myself. I will take my journal to my favorite place on Earth and make it my legend. I will make it my healing out of the old ways and into a new life. I don't know how, yet I know I will manifest a new life.

Yesterday I left the swamps for Colorado. I spent the extra money on a suite with a balcony overlooking the monoliths. I will write from this balcony so much that it will create whatever needs to happen to have my own home here with a window facing the mountains. It's not financially possible today, but somehow and in some unknown way, it will be financially possible another day. I won't leave my children behind. I can't. Yet my heart is at home here and I don't know how to conquer that divide. This journal will be my oak tree, pulling me forth.

There is nothing to fight. Those with faith carry the sword.

With the sun not yet broken over the rock walls, I head to Independence Monument and sit at my favorite spot, with my journal. I see it now, everything is here, leaves, trees, singing, red rocks, light, darkness, solitude, thousands of people asleep to soon awake into this oasis.

I recall an awesome meditation from "Eat, Pray, Love", although it wasn't presented as such. Upon finality of Elizabeth's divorce her friend desperately tries to comfort her. She offers what to me is a truth, one that should be meditated upon. Elizabeth is told to close her eyes and imagine every single person who loves her standing in front of her. The people don't even have to be loved ones; they can be people who just want the best for Elizabeth, as they do for everyone. She tells Elizabeth to hear each of them say that they love her and they want her to be happy. Each of them tells her that it makes them happy to see her in a loving relationship. This is fact. Those who love want others to love. When they express this love, this desire for brightness in everyone's life, they emit from the soul. This is power. In the knowing that we are loved, the best for us is created from the soul. I write down these thoughts and do the meditation.

I open my eyes to a 70-something man standing above me, walking stick in hand.

"I am Albert. This is my favorite spot on Independence Monument. Usually no one is sitting here and I like to be alone but I was drawn to you meditating so I had to come ask who you are."

"I am Rebecca and I've come to this spot to write my memoir."

"Wow! I wrote a book at this spot! This must be why I felt I should talk to you."

We spend another 20 minutes talking about the books and I tell Albert that we should talk again, perhaps here on Independence Monument or over lunch.

"That sounds nice. But people always say they'll meet up again, but they never do. Good bye Rebecca, it was nice meeting you."

We go our separate ways.

The brisk air mingles with the trees outside the open window as I fall asleep. In the distant openness, coyotes bravely sing as they snarl their prey. I assume a mountain lion is out there in the evacuated silence, skulking the rock face in my dark but in her light. The lack of activity, other than the coyotes, sends my mind to create noise. Eyes open, I lie in bed wondering why Paul does not ask for my forgiveness. I wonder if all of the love he placed on me was ever real. I wonder if perhaps I had done something wrong or if my anger kept him at bay.

I feel him now as this faintest breeze resting in my night air.

CHAPTER 10
Symptoms of Fear

Not a single voice or movement from humans, only whispers. Whispers from the faces in the rocks. They speak to the prayers of all those who have come before me. Cactus greens and browns splash the ground for a vast mile in every direction, except for the mighty red rock to my left. My daughter begs me to not hike alone. She left me a text message last evening reminding me of the man who had to cut his own arm off, because he got stuck beneath a rock while hiking alone. I am not alone. The spirits in the rocks talk to me constantly.

Honestly, I'm a little nervous. I'm not 20 years old anymore. Again, I forgot to pack my hiking poles so I grab the largest stick that I can find. I realize there are aggressive animals out here. I've hiked this trail a hundred times, yet today I decide to read the notice at the front of the trail. It includes pictures of black bear, a bobcat and of course, a mountain lion. So now I have fear. So now I will keep looking over my shoulder instead of ahead, exactly the way I do with the corporate sharks. I don't know how to protect myself in the wild, just as I don't know how to protect myself from the man I love.

If I give power to the pain, give strength to betrayal, I will continue to grow in fear and continue to end up where angels fear to tread.

An hour and a half into my hike I see Albert hiking right toward me.

"You said we'd never see each other again," I remind him.

"Well I guess I was wrong. Maybe the Universe wishes us to talk more."

"I still have writing to do this morning, but I'd love to meet you for lunch," I tell Albert with a smile.

"Lunch it is. Let's meet at Subway at 1:00pm."

"It's a date!"

These deep breaths make me feel so alive. I become one with the desert air, with the brush, and most significantly with the red rock monoliths of a thousand faces. I know Spirit is in every piece of Earth around me; I can feel it in the air and see it in the majesty before me. I call out to the faces and they call back. The faces take our prayers and speak them in God's language to the Universe. The energy is so intense it feels as if generations of humans have prayed in this very spot. I can find nothing but love, even for myself. Therefore, I am not alone.

I find a clearing in which to relax and meditate. As feelings of love encompass me, I notice a couple approaching through the brush to my left. I can hear their words before they notice my presence. The woman did not want to take this hike, but her husband wanted it. She expresses to him that she wants to stay home next time. She'd rather be doing laundry. This is a trip for his buddies, not for her.

"You always seem unhappy just sitting at home and tending to the kids. You don't get outside to enjoy life. I thought this would at least be a chance for us to spend time together."

"You know I hate hiking. I'm out of breath and I'd rather be reading a book," the supposed wife responds.

"Well, if you got off of your lazy ass any day of the week, then maybe you wouldn't be out of breath. I bought you that treadmill that you don't use. I'm the one who has to go to work every day. Stop complaining," he screams at her.

They see me. I pretend to not notice. And then, just silence, except for the crackling of branches beneath their hiking boots and the touch of the poles to the rocks.

I bet if she rocked the boat the ripples wouldn't be worth it. I am so happy to be free to choose where I am and who I am.

I return to my hike and head toward my favorite place on the red rock to write. I contemplate

Don't those people feel empty being together? Do I have an emptiness that attracted Paul or did our relationship create the emptiness?

I recall times when I felt full.

Spina bifida and chronic back pain since the age of 12 was one of my first lessons in healing. I refused the back brace that was prescribed. It would have been too embarrassing. However, embarrassment occurred due to one symptom. An abrupt, unexpected flailing. A heated pain would soar up my back so violently, but so quickly, that it didn't have time to leave lasting pain. Yet, it did have time to make my arms and head flail and my knees collapse. Lasting less than a second, the pain was inconsequential. But the flailing was embarrassing because it happened anyplace and at any time. When I got that great-paying job out of college, the one offered at my sister's wedding, taking be back to the South, I did not want this flailing to be seen. But it was seen. So, I began meditating, doing yoga and balancing my energies. I meditated daily on alignment and stillness. I practiced yoga to align my spine. I was full. After six months the pain and the flailing vanished. It has never reoccurred.

So, the gift of healing and balance I could teach others. In every session with clients, I was full.

Later, pregnant with my daughter, I became diabetic and fell significantly ill. When she was an infant I nearly lapsed into a diabetic coma. I was upstairs eating a sandwich at my in-laws house. My husband Michael was asleep in the basement holding Marisha, with Jacob watching TV. Jacob was definitively not allowed to climb the spiraling, sharp-edged stairs, and he never would because he always did as he was told.

I felt sick and thought it was the sandwich. I fell to my knees so very ill that not a single sound came out of my mouth. A catatonic stupor set in and I began to vomit. Horridly and violently my stomach kneaded. After a few minutes my body gave away and I laid in vomit. My mouth gurgled with the rancid puke. The next thing I remember is getting into the car and arriving at the hospital and most especially passing out again in my vomit in the emergency room.

It was only because of my son's individuality and inner knowing that I survived. At two years of age, he climbed those stairs while his dad slept, found his mom and then went screaming to his father. So, screaming isn't always a bad thing. My blood sugar level was at 415 when I arrived at the hospital and I remained hospitalized for three days and couldn't nurse my daughter. That was painful. She cried so hard every time she visited. It was a miracle that I was alive. Jacob had just saved me. I returned home more focused on healing and teaching than ever. I was full.

And now, as I walk beneath the formations of God's voice I can only hear echoes of my own. "*He was such a liar and a cheat. He said he loved me and then he left.*" I catch myself saying out loud, "I want to marry Hugh, no Paul, I meant Paul." *Did I say Hugh? Oh shit, I didn't mean Paul either; he is scum.*

As I make it near Independence Monument by the ancient souls in the rocks, I see my sacred space ahead. If Paul had been here with me now, we would not be here in this sacred space; we would be having a beer.

I lay out my sweater for some cushion, sit with crossed legs and close my eyes. I begin breathing in the stillness and the oneness of this place, allowing myself to relax.

A group of hikers make their way up to MY space and stand behind me. They begin talking of the scene before them. *They could do this from any point on this huge rock, but instead, they decide to interrupt my space. They are so close; I can hear the water gurgling down their throats.* A man explains that it's still afternoon and there is enough time to take on several more miles of hiking. Another has to question if that's the best plans for the day because of happy hour. The women get excited about being able to see so far and ponder where they could go for dinner. They don't shut up, so I decide to turn and give them a little, evil look to remind them that they are standing in my sacred space.

They shut up, but they don't leave.

I try to get settled back into my inner solitude when children begin yelling from below that their mother is lost. They yell to their dad and their dad yells back. "Check the path to the left. I think she turned left!"

Damn it! She's not lost! She's here near Independence Monument. You can't get lost when there is a 500 foot-high beacon to direct your way. No matter how far she wanders, she will see this rock and she can easily find her way back. She is not lost!"

But the kids keep yelling that they will take one hiking trail and their dad should take another in their search. The father agrees, which completely startles me. *Don't they know they should all go to one spot and wait for their mother to return? Are they ignorant?* They don't shut up.

I have lost my ability to meditate. I am so angry. I will just leave early and head back to the hotel to change for lunch with Albert.

As I reach the parking lot, several feelings arise in me. I'm anxious to get back; I feel that I'm in a rush and I don't know what I'm rushing to. The anxiety may be there because I lost Paul, but that means that I have nothing to return to. So, why am I always in a rush to get nowhere?

Am I fearing the best or the worst? What am I running from? What am I running toward?

Yet, I'm still in a rush to something, nervous that I won't get it.

CHAPTER 11

Separation

After spending the entire afternoon with Albert imploring me to contact Paul, because love is all that matters, I just take his thoughts back to the hotel and back to bed.

Lying within the still of the night, absent of human touch, completes my loneliness. I am settled into the place that feels like home, with the window open to the still intensity of the loving earth, yet I can't find the peace to sleep. I am too afraid to contact Paul, because what if he says that I never mattered to him.

I take deep breaths in and out through my mouth recalling that it helps to pretend I am sleeping. I weaken my breath. When I remove the thoughts and pretend to sleep, my body aligns and sleeps. When this doesn't work, I focus on the tip of my nose and only on the tip of my nose. But tonight my attention is elsewhere.

I hear the light wind hit the pillow beneath my cheek. I am so far from my children and so aware of the separation from love in my life. This heaviness stirs my awareness and calming is futile.

I relax my face into the pillow. It enfolds me, holds me and provides a feeling of safety as I try to sleep. The breath on the pillow grows louder. In and out I breathe. Wisp and then a silence, wisp and silence fall across the pillow. It's warmer than I. Then, as I fall more and more still, into the warmth, the sound reflected by the pillow grows louder. Its essence is now out of rhythm with my own breathing. A heavy wisp appears with a storm behind it.

I feel his touch on my shoulder and I don't want to open my eyes. I just want to feel him.

My body falls into the folds of the bed. He presses his warm flesh into my back. His groin moves close and ever so supplely. Lovingly, he takes me in his arms and caresses my back with a cold finger. I fall ever so enraptured by this closeness; aliveness wakens within me, within this bed.

And then our first kiss. It is so tender. It starts slowly with his head drawn around to my face and with a touch from his upper lip. He runs one finger from the base of my neck to the base of my spine. My body gives. Our bottom lips touch and breaths are exchanged. A peck to my lower lip as my mouth remains open. He moves in closer and the kiss grows intense. Our tongues dance in ecstasy.

That finger that just sent waves down my back now reaches between my legs. My mind gives. I have no thoughts, only a compelling desire. My heart beat escalates, although his seems monotone. The electricity circling outside of my body reaches him and I want to feel more of its boundlessness. I go with it and open with the sparks of desire. My desires can't be rescinded. The dam breaks and he easily slides into me. Heat rises with each stroke. My body is completely enraptured. He mounds me. Flashes of sweat pour to the sheets beneath. My body is uplifted, responding to his beat and the crescendos that waft into an ocean of hot, wet, meditative bliss. My wave peaks and crashes to shore.

I awake standing in Dawson's room.

"What are we doing here, Rebecca? You just experienced your opening and yet you land in your distractions," Gashan says disappointedly. "If you try to understand Dawson, you will miss the chance to address your main issue. I took you to Anna to look your separation in the eye. You distract yourself out of cowardice."

"I will address the elephant in the room as soon as I understand this situation," I yell. "I just need to know why Dawson is the object of Anna's affections. I know he is her younger brother, so perhaps he is safety to her, but there is something about him she needs. I just need to understand."

"These are not needs. This is a desire to create another drama that will keep you from your own."

"But Anna is not my drama and I did not ask to go to her."

"I wouldn't be so quick to decide that, Rebecca," Gashan retorts.

Dawson is at his mahogany desk mulling over school work. He hardly notices the knock at the door. A short, plump, male servant of gentle nature enters with a slight bow.

"Mr. Dawson, you will find your night clothes on the back of the chair as always and I have poured you a bath. Your Lordship asks that you get plenty of rest tonight so you may be ready for tomorrow. Lord Kelly is very delighted to take you on your first fox hunt. It seems that he is ready to make you the best heir this region has seen. He talks about it to your mother often."

"But I won't be the heir if mother has a son with Lord Kelly."

"You don't know the future Dawson, so don't project your fears onto it. Don't you want to be the man that your father always imagined? Your father would be delighted to know you as the Lord of such a great estate."

"Yes. I want it more than anything. Father had such an unlucky illness at the prime of his life. He wanted only the best for me and he'd be glad to know that Mother is well supported. I imagine leading this grand estate with honor well into my late years, but I must also ensure that Anna is well kept. Even so, it is the idea of being a Lord that makes me study. It is what I've always wanted."

"I will be back before you blow the candle out, Mr. Dawson."

"Gashan, Anna doesn't realize this desire in her brother. She believes Dawson's main intention is to keep her safe, not to focus on fortune," I explain somewhat mind-shaken.

"Of course it's not about the money, Rebecca. You always make that clear."

"He is a victim as well, Gashan. His father is dead and now his destiny lies within the rules and fate of a strange family."

"Go ahead Rebecca. Go ahead and help him. Tell him what is on your mind. Remind him of his loss. Show him how sorry you feel for him that his father died and left him. Go ahead because I know that is what you want to do. Remind him of his loss. Remind him of his victimhood."

"He is alone and without a father," I scream. "The direction he gets from these people could end in devastation. They don't care what happens to him."

"Then comfort him, Rebecca. Feed his loss. Feed his belief in the death of his father. Feed his belief that he is separated from the soul of his father and you will teach him to create more loss. It would be better if you enlightened him to the fact that he is being controlled by Anna's deep emotions. Devastation will occur if he feeds that darkness."

"How could you be so sarcastic about death and loss, Gashan?"

"That is the question precisely, Rebecca. How could you be? And in what other way could you actually BE?"

My mind spins upon realizing how Gashan turned my own question back on me. I'm dazed. Even out-of-body, I can feel my own anger. In a conscious flash I get the idea, I get that I can be, just be. I can choose happiness, but this makes me angry because I don't feel happiness. But, I get his point. I could be the person who elicits the joy of life, not its disappointments.

"How do we find Anna?" I yell.

"The same way that you find you. Place your attention on that part of yourself that feels lonely."

I turn to find Dawson's door open to a long, lifeless hallway. I step out to its dampness and to internal voices bouncing off the walls. Shouts, from several men, echo off stone at the far end of the hall. That hard, cold stone is like the cramp in the pit of my stomach that appears every time I recall disappointments. But, the voices seem to be hopeful, although the men are inharmonious. Where one man sees a business venture as a means to an end, another sees it as a start, and yet another sees it as a way to power.

I sense my own incongruent thoughts appear. One moment, a relationship is a means to happiness and the next moment it means abuse from a cold-hearted man. Gashan trails nearby and we approach a staircase similar to the one in the servants' quarters, but wider and marked with gold railings.

As we make our way down the stairs, a woman's voice grows near. I'm drawn into the hollowness. I feel as if I'm entering a cave of lies. It's cold. This space is without feeling. Each step downward is a reminder of a deception placed on me. Each step awakens a memory of a lie placed upon me. Abuse. Pure emotional abuse. The woman's voice expands into the pit below.

I am dizzy as I near the end of the downward spiral. A bit of my heart was given to him after each lie, believing it to be the truth. I gave myself away to him and now I am empty.

I leave the last step and peer into a surprisingly well-lit room to see Anna's mother having her hair combed. Several ladies attend to her feet, soaking them in fragrant mint water. Her vanity means nothing to me.

I move from door to door hoping to hear Anna. Instead, the soft, inquisitive voice of Josephine comes through one of the doors. Other rooms are filled with voices of servants tending to women of Aaron's family. None of the doors hold Anna behind them, at least not seemingly.

One young woman expresses guilt over taking Anna's room during her visit. I lean in that direction. Apparently, Anna's room has a better vanity than the rest and the hosts don't want this guest to have anything less. Anna has been placed in a servant's room for the month of August while guests remain in town.

"Let's go to her, Gashan."

I run back up the stairwell to dart across the abbey to the servant's quarters. We don't make it to our destination, as we find

Anna hugging the stone hall of the men's rooms, sneakily opening Dawson's door and closing it behind her. Gashan and I follow.

"I love you so much, Dawson. I can't sleep at night with you so far away. My mind fills with all sorts of fears of what could happen to us here. This is not our family."

"Be calm, dear sister."

"But Dawson, Josephine is prepped each day to find a mate. Suitors are led to her for marriage. She has attended two balls since we arrived and I haven't attended any. Neither mother or Lord Kelly even mention the idea."

"You're being silly Anna. They probably think you don't want to go and they don't want to push you."

"Mother knows how much I love beautiful dresses and only Josephine acquires them. You and I are tucked away at the end of dinner so they may have their secret meetings. They want to set up Josephine to be an heiress. I know they do. We are not the Lord's children and they will ensure that we don't stay here. How are we going to survive, Dawson?"

"I think you are exaggerating sister."

"Then why are we never a part of the discussions and why are we separated from everyone? I've been in the servants' quarters for three weeks now and it gets so cold at night. Papa always made sure that I was warm. Mother will get rid of us like she got rid of Papa."

"Anna! I don't want to hear you say that again. You make me so scared."

"But brother, I know mother poisoned Papa. Just days before he died, I overheard Papa talking to the nurse about Mother having another man. He said he couldn't live the way he was living anymore and that he would prove mother's infidelity. Papa died when we were gone, immediately after that conversation. Mama wanted to get rid of him and she poisoned him."

"Anna, I can't take it," Dawson screams while holding his hands over his ears.

Anna breaks down in tears. Sobbing on her knees she bows her head into the boy's lap. She tries desperately to sob lightly so no one will hear. When Dawson realizes that she is getting out of control, he grabs her, pulls her up to the bed and holds her ever so tightly.

"Dawson, you are the love of my life."

"And you are mine, dear sister."

"Please don't stop holding me; I will break."

With that notion, Dawson asks Anna to hide under the bed while he gets a servant. A short conversation goes on between the two and the man softly blows out the candles and says good night.

Anna escapes from beneath the bed to mount it with a smile that glows brightly by the light of the moon. Her eyes glisten with what were tears of sadness just moments ago. But the gleam now in her eyes reveals how tears turn to relief. She lies down next to Dawson, wrapping him mightily with both arms.

Gashan and I can see everything. The full moon exposes it all.

I shutter for a moment but am afraid that Anna can hear me, so I draw back my sounds and sit quietly in the chair. I feel like a peeping Tom. "Gashan, you should leave. You shouldn't be watching a young girl undress." But, he refuses.

Once the act is over, they fall asleep easily in each other's arms.

I sit still without the ability to change anything. I can't help Anna or Dawson. I am completely powerless. Feelings of isolation wash over me and my longings turn within themselves; the turmoil rises in my stomach. We watch them sleep peacefully with the fear of what will happen next. What will happen next? Says the voice of fear.

Sometime in the deep of the night I am awoken from my stupor when Anna makes off to her quarters. I rise to run after her, but Gashan stops me.

"You should know Rebecca that you don't have to open doors and run to search her out. Just go to her in your heart."

And just like that I am in Anna's room watching her lie in bed wide awake.

I can read her thoughts. She is remembering her father in a

Library with her nurse. She recalls the conversation where her father vowed to prove that his wife was cheating. And, she skips forward to finding her father dead after a week at her aunt's house. She sees her mother with a doctor and housemaid standing over him. But then her face tweaks in confusion at the scene of a woman leaving on horseback through the woods. She saw it through her window. She thinks that the woman is involved in her dad's death, along with her mother.

Anna's thoughts jump to Dawson and the terrible things that could happen if her mother found out about their intimate love. She doesn't care what her mother thinks, because she hates her. They can throw her and Dawson out. They will survive; they will always have each other. They can make it back to France and live at their aunt's house. They can handle anything as long as they are together. If her mother tried separating them, this wouldn't matter because Dawson would always find her. He is so smart and able. He is so strong at heart and mind that he would go from village to village until he found his loving sister.

The sun rises sooner than she would like, as she still lies awake embodying a storm of thoughts. Her body is heavy from the lack of sleep and this obviously makes her sadder. She holds her head down while getting dressed for the day and a desperate look of solemnity covers her soul.

When she feels ill she feels sad, and when she feels sad, her body feels ill. Neither are the true source of the disturbance.

As the servants are busy preparing the quarters for weekend guests to the ball, it is easy for Anna to steal a moment away with Dawson. He is in his room with his studies when she arrives. She checks to ensure that Mr. Knightly is gone from the men's quarters and quickly slides a chest behind the door.

"I am so tired, Dawson. I didn't sleep a bit after we separated last night. Could you help me to nap for just a little while?

Dawson reluctantly slides under the covers with her but he holds her oh so lovingly. He kisses her on top of the head and rubs her arm like she desires. It calms her down and releases her tension. She begins caressing him and slides her hands under the covers. The kissing begins.

"Sister, I love you. I want you to be happy. Papa is gone, but I am not."

He brushes her head with his fingers, from crown to the base of her neck. He kisses her neck in this same spot that his hand had stopped and then softly rolls over on top of her.

The leather straps of the bed are swooning and one abrupt move makes the legs of the bed creak.

The door barrels open, shoving the chest to land at my feet. I scream. It is Aaron's father, Lord Brown.

"I was hoping this was not what I suspected, but this is the second time I have seen you enter this room Anna! I cannot keep this a secret from my dearest old friend."

He leaves two startled teens frozen in the bed. Anna's breasts are exposed and Dawson politely covers them.

"You must go back to your room now, Anna" exclaims Dawson.

My emotions whirl for these troubled kids. I have to follow Anna. I know that this could mean ruin.

"Gashan, the poor child is only acting out her feelings of isolation and pain. She doesn't feel that anyone loves her other than her brother. The one man who did love her was killed by her mother. I have not seen one person in this estate come ask about her well-being. She's just acting out a desperate need for love."

My emotions, my fears grow so very intense. I begin running toward the servants quarters to find Anna's door, but can't find myself to be able to enter. I am so fearful of what I will see. This kind of pain of people letting you down, of regrets and angst can cause immeasurable suffering and I don't want to be reminded of my own.

I fall to the hall floor and weep. I weep until the thoughts of my own longing are removed because the need to remove Anna's suffering is larger.

I am suddenly in a dark, cold room lit by the candles that the Lord holds in his hand. He and Mr. Brown stand over Anna.

"Mr. Brown returns to Ireland in one week and you will go with him. You can take all of your clothes and essentials. I will give Mr. Brown the money for your good care until you are married. You will find a man in Ireland, I am sure. Your mother does not need to know any more details. I will ensure her of your care and you can write to her and to her alone after one year. In this time I am certain that you will come to understand the gravity of your deeds."

And just as quickly as I had appeared, the Lord and Mr. Brown are gone, leaving a weeping girl to lie on the cold floor hugging the leg of a chair.

Inside her locked room, Anna's body is hungry but she can't eat. Her nurse has brought several trays of food over the last few days, but Anna just turns away. Only a few bites of muffins has she been able to swallow.

She sometimes lashes out at the walls that surround her. "They have done this to me! They killed father and took us from home only to separate me from Dawson. If they would have just left us in Rennes, Dawson and I would have been happy and would not have to endure their lifeless games. Our aunt would have loved us."

Anna lies on the bed weeping and holding her stomach. She imagines how Dawson might be locked in his room without food or perhaps how her mother is poisoning him. Oh, the pain he could be enduring with poison. Their mother is so evil; Dawson will never escape her wrath.

As she stares at the ceiling she exclaims out loud, "They can't keep us apart; we will find each other. I will just be in Ireland, dear brother. Across the water. You will reach me there; I know that you will."

In this isolation her mind creates scenarios far separate from the reality of the happy abbey readying itself to bid farewell to the guests. The ball goes off brilliantly and Josephine and Aaron are soon to be engaged. It was apparent on their faces by the last dance of the evening, in which he hadn't taken another hand.

The prison that Anna's room has become has also become her. She is cold and still, holding a soul inside that is void of trust or belief in the world.

As her day of leave approaches, the sorrow, longing, isolation and confusion turn to rage. She knows no other than what she has witnessed with her eyes, her father's concerns, her mother's coldness, her lack of a family to comfort her. The rage explodes as tremors of screaming and night sweats, with no one responding. She hits the walls, screams at her isolation, screams at her winch for a mother, screams at God and how He would make us so separated from love and comfort. "How can no one understand? Why have I lost my father? Where is Dawson? A loving God would never approve of this isolation!"

Her hands are bleeding from the blows to the stone. I run to comfort her, taking her into my arms and she bows her head into my shoulder. What is she imagining now? Who does she think she is leaning on?

Slight solemn washes over her and then her sobbing breaks to a few puffs and tears. She lies back down and quickly falls asleep.

I sit next to her on the bed pondering her longings for love and how she has come to be so unsafe at such an early age. She is isolated from love and her acts isolated herself. She is separated from those who have loved her and this pain reaches so deeply into my being.

The heaviness of these thoughts lays me down on the bed beside her, quickly falling asleep, only to wake, slowly, step-by-step in rousing realizations of my addiction to loss. Bit by bit my mind throws together symbols and dreams and ideas of who I could be if I had not been attracted to loss, attracted to the pain in a man so similar to my own.

Realization after realization awakens me until my eyes open that I am late for my flight out of Colorado.

CHAPTER 12
Cowardice

During my layover in Salt Lake City I can't believe my eyes. It's Hugh, my Hugh, boarding a connection flight. He looks back before entering the deck way, as if he's missing something and our eyes meet. He issues a gentle smile and a conciliatory, sweet nod; only to be returned with my wide-eyed smile, beaming 'Don't I look great? I am so happy without you!'

It's been over a decade and we live only 10 miles apart; yet, I haven't seen him until now, and 1,500 miles away. Here I am with my chance to recognize the sweetness in our souls; yet, I can't get over my ego enough to give him the same gentle, loving smile that he offers me.

I'm not in love with him anymore. I'm not even attracted to him. There are no tingles in my body. *Then, why do I have to pretend that I am happier than him? Why don't I just acknowledge the love for what it was and be happy with that gift?* We truly loved each other. Our separate worlds had to be tended to, his to his now wife and step-sons and mine to my babies. It's our creations that kept us apart, not our love. Love is why we recognized one another.

I make it home late at night to realize how much my body is begging for a massage. I don't journal. It's too late. I sit down for a cigarette because it still has its hold on me. It keeps me from breathing in life, from dealing with my reality, all of my creations.

Understanding Anna's reality, I will better know my own. I want to help her, to heal her pain. She needs hope of a good life with love and comfort ahead. She is not my creation. She once lived. Somewhere inside I know that we can heal the past.

I call Dora to exchange these most recent happenings. She is excited to connect again after so many weeks. There is so much to talk about, so many dreams to relay. We are both ready for bed but figure that a good talk with laughter will begin this week on a good note.

"I feel carefree right now, Dora. I know that the universe is working for me. I'm letting go of those past hurts. Guess who I ran into at the Salt Lake City Airport?"

Dora sees the sighting of Hugh as a sign. "Your spirit guides made this happen. You wanted him to give up everything for you and now you aren't even attracted to him. You wanted him to cross an ocean for you and you believed that you would not be happy without him. And you have moved on, just like you will with Paul. You should ask yourself why this reoccurs in your life. Do you think Hugh is Dawson?"

"Probably. I wish I could have just given him a pleasant smile."

"Rebecca, you have disconnected from Source. You are unconsciously trying to get his energy by not being nice. This is the same that you are doing with Paul. Isn't that what most relationships are about, getting energy from each other?"

"Oh, yes, I forgot about that Dora," I respond.

"Rebecca, I think I know what is happening here. May I explain?"

"Of course."

"You are scared of your greatest gifts. You are afraid to walk your path because you fear an ending like that with Hugh and Paul. Disappointment. Yet, you have things backwards! When you disconnected from Source and entered the corporate world, you were still being urged to walk your path. So, your world keeps reminding you of everything that you are not! Paul is the reminder. Walking your path is the goal and the results will be beautiful. Walking your path brings your spirit into your body and you are full. You are full of energy, of life and spirit. Then you will meet a partner who is also full, so you can share in a true partnership. You have unconsciously been trying to get this energy from relationships when all along the energy is all around you as the presence of Source. Once you rely on that energy and once you are full again, you will have the partnership of your dreams and you will no longer feel a longing. It is the connection to spirit that you are after and you find that by using your gifts!"

The understanding seeps deeply within my soul and I know to turn my focus to love, the embodying of spirit within my body. Dora and I continue to talk and laugh. We talk of silly things we have done together; we talk about my ex-boyfriends and her ex-boyfriends. We make fun of their toupees, their laziness and our stupidity for loving them. I drift into silence immediately and sleep well.

I awake early enough to get some of my journaling done before returning to work. I sit and write my experiences with Anna and the abbey. I write down the words 'isolation', 'separation', 'longing'. I feel them in myself and take this moment to meditate on them and release them.

My entire day is filled with nervousness. I don't know why. I regularly look over my shoulder and feel distracted in meetings. I don't accomplish much because my mind moves in a thousand directions. I sit at my desk for maybe 10 minutes at a time before I head to the restroom, or get a glass of water, or search for an answer to a question from someone on the other side of the building. At the end of the day, my body and my mind are completely exhausted. I can feel my shoulders slouch and my head droop as I carry my laptop down the wide, dimly lit hallway that is decorated with a modest brown and green carpet. This is a dull existence.

And then, of course, my phone beeps. It is a message from Paul. "I see you down the hallway, you look great! I am in town for the weekend to visit my girls." I hate his ways. I hate how he tries to manipulate me into talking to him so that he will feel like a big man. I walk out the door without acknowledging his message. I don't respond, but it eats at me as I travel home.

Even over a lovely dinner with my children, I can't stop bringing the TEXT into my mind. I listen to Marisha's concerns over the amount of books she has to read for English class and at Jacob's request to take him to his next baseball tournament, but I can't get Paul's manipulations out of my head. The recognition that I allowed him to manipulate me is painful.

The living room is quiet because Jacob plays his video games with head phones. Marisha does her homework as I search for answers from my inner self.

I know what I can do. From a compound fracture to my right hand, my dominant hand, 15 years ago, I learned that writing with my left hand opens a portal to unconscious knowledge. I grab my journal and with my left hand I write "What was the spark that created today's nervousness?"

The pen starts moving and the word '*Craziness*' appears. '*The mind is too active and is looking for too many possibilities. You're going outside peace. Rebecca and Dora talked too much last night about their pasts. Rebecca triggered too many thoughts that are disconnected from the soul. Rebecca and Dora laughed at the shortcomings of others. You sparked your disappointments by seeing disappointments in others. Focus only on Source. View others as God would view them.*"

I stare into my wall that I decorated so many years ago, but have neglected since. The paint is no longer white and the green reeds still adorn the Asian fan, but they no longer capture this space. It doesn't hold the same beauty. It doesn't enliven me. It has grown pale. The dust and hints of grey are obvious and remind me of all of my neglecting tendencies, especially toward myself.

I recall recent times where I triggered my state of mind the evening before. One day after an evening of watching my favorite sitcom, and just laughing before going to sleep, my car battery died on the way home from work. I was twenty miles from home with no one to help. Any other day, I would have been anxious as hell. Not this day. I was not nervous and felt to call my son. Jacob called his friend who lived only two miles from where I was parked. The mother appeared in just ten minutes, drove me to a nearby auto store, and even replaced my battery on her own. Like an angel, she just did it without question. She said that we should be of service to others. And throughout the entire experience I felt completely at ease that all would be taken care of. I had fallen asleep the night before in lightness.

Yet after another evening when I had read a couple chapters from a new best seller before hitting the bed, my experience was detrimental. In the book, a young woman entered a chamber filled with sadomasochist paraphernalia. Whips hung from a cross and handcuffs decorated the walls. My dream world was filled with unbelievable images of babies' chained by the ankles and wrists. In my dream, these babies were being directed as if they were puppets. Each baby had a master above them pulling their strings. One man, holding a cross in his right hand, demanded the strings that hung from each corner to move left and right, up and down, until the babies were mangled.

I was a useless the following day.

My consciousness is filled with images, images from history books and war movies, images from the feelings inherited from my family and the longings that I have experienced. A desolate heart and a hanging Jesus must mean so many things to this mind. If I focus on the love and compassion within my heart, I know that I will grow stronger. I will be happy and my children will know better how to create a life of happiness because they deserve it, as we all do.

I unconsciously wake up with a scream out "Paul!" And he is still not lying next to me, yet my soul feels him in my dreams. And

I remember the dream from which I just awoke and must write it down:

I was carrying a striking white, silk gown. It was a wedding gown.

The moment was to be beautiful; it was my creation. A blank page. A blank, beautiful piece of silk. It flowed through the air.

The wedding was to take place on ice and snow. My fiancé and I were going to slide down the ice to the altar, to our love. My friends were there. Everyone was happy. The snow and ice were semi-sculptures. They weren't perfect and they weren't organized. But they were our ice sculptures, of dolphins and roses and hearts and they were perfect for our intentions of creating love and beauty. They were created as a symbol of the beauty, of sliding into the blank page of our future together. No worries.

Then, my mom appeared. She screamed, "No!" She didn't like that the ice wasn't organized. She saw it only for the function that it had. She saw that it wasn't perfect; not that it was a simple beauty. She didn't see that it was created from peace, purity and love.

She said no. She said that I wasn't pretty enough in this setting, and that the ice wasn't pretty. She wanted a church with wood seats and real flowers.

I reacted and I reacted strongly. I reacted because I knew she had the power to stop the wedding. She did stop the wedding. She interrupted the beauty. Her disappointment caused the ice to melt in the exact spot that I was supposed to slide down the ice, slide down to my love.

I reacted. I disfigured the white silk, coloring it with every color of marker that I could find. I was so angry. I yelled. I screamed. I burst out into total emotion.

She ruined my wedding. I fear things will be ruined. I fear that I'll disappoint others. Fear has taken ahold of me and I had no idea.

My reactions have set up a shield that I'm breaking through. I reacted to Paul violently when he left me. Is it my violent reactions and my shield that is keeping love at bay?

I should exercise, but I won't. I want to conquer my unhappiness, but I don't know where to start. In my dream I did not stand up to my mother; in my life I'm not standing up to Paul.

Thoughts arise in my mind; each bringing its own distinct feeling into my heart, into my gut and into my nerves. I shake as I make my way to the coffee machine. I've been running from Paul for well over a year. My heartache remains the same. Anguish over the inability to understand how he could lie to me repeatedly. Anguish over my delusion. Hatred in the recollection of his voice telling me that I'm the love of his life. He travelled with me, danced with me and held my hand always spurting the words that we are together forever. And in the end, it was all words.

My anger expands and I can't get to a glass of wine fast enough. Then I become mad at the fact that I own this anguish. I shouldn't have any feelings of love for him; I shouldn't miss someone who took my feelings for granted. It is so much easier to hate him. So I do. I sit and remember all of the reasons for hating Paul. *I can't miss the love of a liar and a cheat. He's weak, he's not honest. He continued the lie in his own selfishness, not caring about all of the people it would hurt when they discovered his true essence. He is a coward!*

So many memories return to my head. Times of him stepping out of the room for what was supposedly a business call. The hundreds of times that we ate dinner near his wife's house, oh yes, his house. What would he have done if his wife had walked in? *He would have probably smiled because he imagined two jealous women. That thought must have made him feel great.* At the very end, someone did walk into one of our dinners and I've never seen someone run so quickly out.

My anger turns to rage. Who is ruining my wedding? A rancid longing rips at my gut, creating a void that can't be filled. I'm so angry at myself for not seeing the truth.

With the third glass of wine I text him, "You selfish son-of-a-bitch. How could you lie to someone who gave you their heart? You are an abusive man, especially to your wife. The fact that she puts up with it means you deserve one another."

My angry tone either shocks him or gives him an opening to call me.

The conversation begins mostly with my yelling. Screaming that includes hateful words as I stand in my kitchen with my hand on my hip feeling all of my hate directed toward him. "You have a serious problem! You have lived your life in a lie and easily can look someone in the eye and lead them on with false hope, going home to your wife to do the same."

"You're right, Rebecca. I know I had a problem. I have tried to heal it. I want to be a good person and I'm sorry that I lied to you. I am so scared of hurting people that I hide the truth from them. It hurt me to not address my feelings and I felt dead inside when you left. I know that I messed up. But I have moved on and have been doing the right thing." And the thought occurs to me that I am fearful of hurting people; I am fearful of disappointing my parents. I don't address my true feelings for fear of punishment. Perhaps I am a coward.

Then, he begins to cry. It seems like a very sincere cry.

This makes him my prey. He is now broken and I can go in for the kill. I am now the coyote and he is the rabbit. I will tear him to pieces.

I keep drinking and my anger grows. I had really wanted to hear him say that he isn't a liar and that I had misjudged the entire event. I wanted him to tell me that everything he ever said was true but that his wife has cancer and he had to go back to take care of her.

But no, he admitted that he was a liar. He admitted exactly what I have been calling him for years and I can't handle it. "You're a sick man! You son-of-a-bitch!" And the name calling gets worse. I hang up once I realize how far my words had gone.

Paul calls in the evening when I am feeling terrible from the wine and about the words that I had said. I am so regretful of the words. My negative, degrading reaction hurt me more than anything he said to me. This is the perfect time for him to call because my body is filled with regret. Perhaps I have made yet another mistake.

My mind turns to all of the reactions that I have had over the years, the ones that Michael describes as keeping people at bay. Perhaps Paul didn't know how to talk to me because he feared such a strong reaction from me. I agree to meet him for dinner.

I listen to Paul and cry silently until I decide that I can no longer heal the longing alone. The feelings of separation from him are so intense, so painful that I can't eat on many days. I can't be isolated from him anymore and be a healthy person. In this moment I agree to trust him, and allow him the space to do as he needs to do.

Paul explains that he wants to move back home and that he still sees us having a future together. He seems sincere and explains that his divorce is final yet there is much he needs to take care of in Atlanta so we will take everything one day at a time until he returns. I come home to a peaceful bed and restful sleep.

I awake without pain and with a sense of calm within my being. I realize how much inner peace dictates my physical condition and I think that if I can learn to just have peace wherever I am at in life, that perhaps I would always feel good. I realize that if all of my words were peaceful, then perhaps I would always feel good.

I recall my dream that seemed to still be occurring as I was waking up. I was in a 2-story yellow house which sat above a sparkling-blue lake. Both Sara and Tim were inside the home with me. Sara handed me a newspaper with a picture of the book "Creating Forward" and then Tim pointed to the big letter 'S' on his shirt and said "This is your future business, Rebecca."

They took me outside to peer at the lake that now looked more like an ocean. It was vast. Blue, still water in which I could see to the bottom. Whales were everywhere. Large whales, gray whales, I saw two humpbacks swim over the top of the others. They swam slowly without the need to do anything other than just be.

The tide receded and the whales exited as an ancient city was revealed. Hundreds of people appeared with rakes and shovels and other tools to rebuild the ancient city. Tim explained that these people had done this for me many times before.

It is this ancient wisdom that we are supposed to be uncovering. We have helpers in which we should be standing in gratitude. If I were only to focus on my inner truths and work toward this future business, my emotions would be clear and calm like the waters that held the whales.

I realize that it has been many weeks since I've seen Gashan. I realize that feelings of love and trust make me healthy and bring me visits from Sara. I realize that worry drives me the opposite direction, to Anna and to scream for healing within myself. Perhaps both work, but I sure feel better with the visits from Sara.

Paul texts me daily to remind me of his love. I have good days and I have bad days. On the bad days, there is a hunger, a longing in my stomach and it is difficult to be active or to be around friends. On good days, I feel alive and happily participate in my children's lives.

I decide to do a little more manifestation by booking a room at the South Beach Biloxi Hotel in Mississippi for the weekend. I will sit by the window and write while looking out at the ocean. I will work on my book as I take in the beauty of Mother Nature, just as I am meant to do from my future home in Colorado. And as I book the room, I receive an email from Paul. He is in town but cannot visit with me on this occasion. Perhaps we will see each other at work when he stops by Friday afternoon.

As I head to work with my luggage in tow, looking forward to leaving early to get to the ocean, I have a thought, a suspicious thought. And therefore, I turn my car around and head north to Paul's favorite golf course. I wait. It only takes 45 minutes before he arrives, with his two girls, with a buddy, and with his new girlfriend.

CHAPTER 13
The Elephant Acknowledged

My numb limbs break into the bed. The give in the mattress is not enough to comfort my burning flesh. Again, nothing resides inside of me.

I allow myself to make this same mistake, trust, over and over and over again. The shock both deadens me and stirs me. My nerves don't know to give up or to fire. And again my anger makes me too rustled to sleep.

Plumes of dust are kicked up in my thundered march down the stairs to grab a bottle of wine. Grasping the bottle by the neck and a glass by its tail, I approach the stairs to return to that space that keeps drawing me back, my lonely bed shadowed by the menacing tree. But, I can't make it back up the stairs. The anger burning out of nothingness wants to share itself with others.

I throw the blinds back in hopes to see life outside. Perhaps someone will give me comfort, or someone will take the burns of this explosion. I can't make it to the ocean and the lights are out in my neighbors' homes. Everyone is preparing for another day with a deep rest.

I now recall why I deadened myself years ago. I recall why I said 'NO' to love. My body could not digest what it did not understand and therefore it got sick. And therefore, I quit love. Love had hurt me and I went on for over a decade, fine without being completely alive. And now, after returning to love and trust, and having a relationship that went well past the infancy stage, I am left to starve to death. Since Paul knew he was lying all along, he has no death to absorb, I am left absorbing a dying child.

I pour a second glass of wine and somehow make it to the bedroom. But, I can't lie down. I first hold my face in my hands as I push myself into the high chrome rails of my bed. The pain on my shoulders is nothing to the pain in my heart. My left hand trembles as it brings the glass to my mouth.

I sit and drink until this glass is finished and then fall into the fetal position on my left and then on my right. There isn't a comfortable position, neither on my stomach nor on my back. I pull the covers over me to elicit stillness, but this only brings me to violently kick them off.

As I throw myself up to sit bowed over on the side of my bed, tears begin to form as the anger burns. I don't understand. I can't believe it. I don't know to whom I should be the angriest. Me or him? My fingers find their way to my hairline and pull, just pull. My palms start at the corners of my eyeballs and push the scalp upward, pulling the skin with it. I feel the skin on my nose tauten. I know what my face must look like, the bold, obscured, angry one that resides inside. *Who can I be mad at? Why am I here again? Why the anger, again?*

My head falls to my knees and my elbows point to the floor. *Unbelievable. Why do I believe in people?*

I head back downstairs to get drunker. I'm already dead inside, so what will more drunkenness hurt? It will numb the pain that already numbs me.

The cold hardwood floor outside of my tiny bathroom is uncomfortable, but it holds me and makes me more acutely aware of my bones that are breaking with my heart. I really begin to cry. I don't need a soft bed; this hardness is what I lie in all of the time.

Tears fall and anguish deepens. *I've been forging the wrong path;*

I should have given all of my love to my children and not to any man.
Silence ascends from that hole inside of me, my thoughts stop and
blankness is before me. My nails take one last dig deep into my scalp,
bringing to me an acute awareness of my pain. The pain again guides
me to unconsciousness.

Tears on the mangled wood cannot be heard. They are only felt
as cold wetness added to an already moist air. Anna's head hangs
back into the crevice between a leather door and a wooden seat.
Tears are drowning the seat in which her body is folded. It's chilly,
yet she is wearing a loose smock that hangs from her breasts to her
ankles. Her arms are bare, yet a blanket lies at her feet. She is numb.
There is nothing for her to believe in. She is lost, broken and unable
to recover.

It is getting dark outside and the caravan is positioned out of
my view. But I can hear the stomps of what sounds like ten or more
horses. We are amongst a brigade. As I rest to sit in the seat across
from Anna, I recognize Aaron next to me, with his eyes locked on
Anna. He has compassionate eyes, but doesn't lift the blanket to
cover her thin-framed body. Her socks have fallen and barely cover
her ankles. Lifeless, except for the tears, her body doesn't shift but
her head makes a few involuntary jerks.

I want to cover her up, to keep her warm.

Aaron, at a loss for what he is witnessing, addresses Anna. "I
can't recall seeing a woman in such despair. It is more typical to have
gladness over going off to find a husband. Once you are settled, I
am sure you will love our home and the village. Your family is just
a few days away and they will visit soon."

A long pause absorbs us.

"Do you really miss your family this much, Anna? It has only
been hours. Is it the abbey or is it a fear of living with our family, in
an unknown place?"

No recognition from Anna.

"I regret not spending some time with you while we were in
Derby. It seemed there was never a chance. I rarely saw you at

banquets and never saw you at a ball. Don't you like to dance? There is hope ahead, Anna. Many young suitors are teaming near the docks. And they are getting wealthy with the goods we ship to America. You will visit the village, the gatherings for women and book-readings. I am certain that mother will dress you well."

The carriage comes to an abrupt halt in the center of a village road. The voice of Mr. Brown is loud and presumptuous when he exclaims to new voices that his family must be sheltered and fed for the night. Movement escalates as is apparent by the scattering of stones and handling of doors and women and horses.

Aaron just keeps his eyes locked on Anna as if he expects her to make a startling leap from the trap door, which then abruptly opens. Mr. Brown and a snarling of arms grab reach to Anna, to withdraw her from the carriage. She does not resist. They don't ask for her hand, but instead scoop her up amongst the folds of their coats and whisk her away.

Her potential demise is in front of me. I grab onto her smock, attaching myself to her fate. A broad man, draped in a brick red cape and white stockings, cups Anna in his arms, while Lord Brown stays to the right and Aaron to the left. The distance to which Aaron gives Anna allows me to nestle between them and hold on.

A man brushes the dirt away from the front of his variety shop. He offers tea, but Mr. Brown declines. Mrs. Brown stands beneath a gas light with her daughters who are all dressed in hourglass gowns beneath brown shawls. Anna is gently let down in their care as the women throw a blanket around Anna's shoulders and lead her by the arms.

"Anna, you must get angry! You must get angry to break out of this prison," I yell falling on deaf ears. "If you have despair, locked up emotions, anger will help!"

My eyes pare the penetrating darkness enclosed by stone slabs in this narrow alley. My sight lands in the distance on a woman holding a candle and standing in a doorway motioning with a yank of her flabby arm to continue toward her.

I just wish Anna would awake. I wish she didn't expect doom with this departure from her brother. She can have love again and she will see Dawson again. Love is a definite. It is what pulls us all forth. It is the destination of all. Her measured walk and lifeless stature frightens me.

"Get angry, Anna! Save yourself, Anna! Stand up and say that you deserve better. Get angry to get unsnarled from these tangled emotions."

The gas lights behind us are as small as nits as the lady before us grows larger, filling the doorway in which she stands on the other side of the crossing road. I hear Mrs. Brown reminding the girls that the carriages will be ready promptly at sunrise.

We approach the crossroads where a lonesome shadow lurks. The arms of the shadow reach from behind the stone building. Then, in a flash, the scrawny, yet daunting figure lunges outward from behind the corner. He remains on his knees, in the dirt, holding what glistens like a metallic mug at Anna's knees. He's a drunkard. His whisky sweat evaporates into the cool night air. The smell sweet, yet obtrusive.

"I lost my flute and all means of playing to my audience," he screams. "Provide me with some hope. Some tokens, please," he begs and screams louder as he holds his mug upward and begins to stand. "Just one token, please!"

As they walk on, the bum lunges forward and grabs Anna's blanket and then her smock. The blanket removed and the smock ripped down the nape of her back reveals her frailness and the bones that are beginning to protrude from beneath her skin.

"I need tokens to reach my family and I need tokens to buy a new flute. I get paid in Derby and in London with my flute concertos."

The women shudder, trying to pretend he doesn't exist.

"You have tokens to offer a poor man but you don't give them! You are a winch!"

The broken, desperate Anna before me cracks open, her anger unleashed. Turning while raising her arms and voicing a guttural charge against this drunkard, Anna belts out at the desolate man, slashing his face with her nails, pounding his cheeks and pulling his thick, black hair with her fingers. The women struggle to unclasp her grip as the bum falls back to the ground, face in stone and dirt.

"I will eat you for dinner!" the spirit between Anna's teeth violently exhales.

I am in shock. I said those words once. Those exact words. That same unleashed anger once resided inside of me. I can't move. I just stare into darkness, aware of the gowns brushing one another as they shroud Anna, ushering her to the old woman a few steps away.

The door opens and then slams shut. The women are gone.

I lean against the gray stone and feel my own sense of hopelessness that I've engendered repeatedly in my life, seemingly because I don't let my feelings be known. I fall to the cold ground and wish I had that pathetic man's mug of beer.

We sit together, a flute's length apart. We both weep inside but tears do not awaken. We are strangers in the night, feeling heavy by the hands we were dealt in life.

His heavy breathing saddens me. His Anguish over loss is inconsolable.

Anguish.

Is love only meant for some? Is loss our own doing, or is loss God's calling through longing for us to find Him? Will I ever have a peaceful, trusting relationship that fills me with joy? Will this man's fortune ever be restored?

I am drawn to sit closer to him, closer to his despair. This is not because I want his comfort, I want to comfort him. I feel his pain. I know loss.

I slide to his right arm and stare ahead into the dark wall of this passage. A sweet musk of sherry and tobacco pierce my every inhalation. But still, I sit near this man feeling stronger than him, stronger than Anna, and knowing that I must help Anna, if only I can understand what is required.

Staring into nothingness, the reality of what just happened is apparent. Anna unleashed a tremor of anger that was buried. The monster-like sound from her mouth was the voice of the collective anguish. The voice of a lurking shadow created by anguish. But I only called for that simple anger, that which demands our boundaries to be built. I wanted her only to release the despair and energy that keeps her separate from love.

Pain can become attachment and in attachment, we get lost. Then, we believe the pain, and with belief the pain has us. Pain lurks in the shadows.

With this sense, I lean into this sad man and become still. I begin to drift into his breathing, into his despair. In and out his chest gurgles and the smoke plays a dense song as it whistles through his teeth. At least it is not winter.

The lady in the house opens a window and fills this narrow corridor with the aromas of stew and potatoes. The heat melts my nostrils and weighs on my memories of eating in my grandmother's kitchen. Poor in money but rich in heart, my grandmother served banquets daily from her garden. Too poor for beef as the main course, she would shred small portions of meat into a potato broth with onions, carrots and peas. To accompany this, there were always cucumbers in vinegar, stewed tomatoes, cornbread, raspberries, that she had likely canned a year or more prior, and molasses. Sweet molasses.

I ride up into these sweet tastes in life that are wafting out of the windows and down this narrow street in happy childhood memories of sharing love.

I must bring that sharing of love back into my life. Other memories just haunt. I don't know when I separated myself from the feast. I could have made good relationships and built them up even better, but no man has met my expectations. No man has met the expectations of my mother.

The dark alley expands and contracts with the chest of the bum. He sleeps to forget the day, but these walls don't forget him. They enclose him and echo back each utterance from his lips. A bitter cold wind swoops down into the floor between these walls and catches my skin.

Oh, yes, I remember this dark alley. This is the bitter cold, dark alley behind my college dorm room. I was just trying to get to the library to study for my economics final before the sun came up. The snow slowed my steps and the wind bit at my nostrils. I had to keep my face down to keep the wind from stinging my eyes.

Approaching a large row of skeleton bushes a man jumped in my path and placed the pocket of his coat to my neck, explaining that the knife inside his pocket would slit my throat if I screamed. It wouldn't have mattered if I screamed. It was 4:30am and all of the lights were out in the single dormitory that stood in this far reach of campus. Everyone slept while I panicked and froze. He named my sisters and my brother; he named my parents. He had been stalking me, but I had been unaware. He threatened my life and that of my family. He attacked me there in the snow. I don't recall anything of the following six months. But, I do recall the reactions I received when I tried to get help.

Months later, after finally talking to campus officials about the incident, they shut me up. When telling my professors that I was going through emotionally hard times and needed a little leniency, they gave me none. When needing money to eat, because I was unable to work from the grief over those six months, I asked my parents for help. The request was denied. They thought that I was drinking their money away. I continued to eat the hotdogs that my roommate left in the refrigerator.

That is when I started to drink. This was the elephant left unacknowledged.

Lucidity. Staleness. Aching. Aloneness. Why should I feast with betrayers? I couldn't trust anyone.

Oh yes. This is when the bad relationships started. This is when I began attracting men I couldn't trust.

I don't have to live in that identity anymore. It is past. It is gone. My life should be the one that I came here to live. My path should be the one that my Native American guide willed to me while standing in front of my childhood bed. "You will, Rebecca. You will do your spiritual duty. You will."

I've crossed the abyss, stood with Masters, healed myself and seen Heaven and my own little Hell. I can guide people through the depths of despair.

I see this battle clearly. It is one that I'm created to win.

I choose to create myself out of this darkness. I need to get back home, back to Rebecca and be the spiritual author that my life has been fighting to become. Any other choice leads to death of the myriad of purposeless creations that I've exacted. Those deaths are suffering. I should not be tangled in them. But, how do I get home?

"What year is it?" I ask the lucid man.

"1845."

His voice startles me and I turn in intrepid realization to two arms reaching toward me, the right one holding a mug and the other banishing a flute.

"Gashan!"

"My dear Rebecca, you look surprised. Didn't you need me? You left without me. Did you notice? You didn't need me this time. This time, it was not Anna you were looking for; it was me." And he stares with blazing eyes that turn from desire to anger, as if I had betrayed him.

"No, Gashan. I want to help Anna. She is crushed and I understand her pain. I know it can be healed before she creates her entire life upon this separation."

"You won't be able to help her until she knows you are here and you won't be able to make yourself known here in this time until you sleep with me."

"What does that mean, Gashan?" I see him with fear for the first time since I've known him.

"Understand that we are neither being nor nonbeing. We come from everywhere at once. Showing yourself in 1845 just depends on using the energy behind your breath to put your existence here. To

119

find that energy behind your breath, you need to reach orgasmic heights of ecstasy and relinquish all that Rebecca knows, falling into this world. I am here to show you."

"Anna rested her head on my shoulder just weeks ago. She knew I was there, her head fell over in relief when she realized my presence. I already know how to transcend these boundaries that you believe ecstasy takes care of."

"You need a man Rebecca. Remember? You've spent your life looking for the 'right' man and identifying your happiness based upon him. Fall into our relationship and we will help Anna escape her prison together."

And with that, Gashan puts down the mug and raises his flute to his mouth to begin seducing me with sounds that are riddles lying in ecstasy.

Flutters are sent out from the flute and into my heart. The flutters tap the energy around my head and spin out of control in my heart as love, and love is all I can image. The concerto is brilliant, tingling all of my extra senses from tongue to lap, but it is so very, very cruel.

Tear drops bounce through my chest and the notes spin in my head, heightening then falling. Cresting then flowing. In the distance I hear a clap along with the beat. Hands slapping on knees. The sounds echo off the stone walls and then bounce off of our bodies. The melody dances in my head. Swift high notes titillate my ears and then fall into my gut. A dance of love is actual and then sad, once given and then taken away, spins my reality.

He repeats this dance of love that expounds happiness then turns it to loss and then to anguish. It's all too familiar and so easy to be submerged within.

Whirling around me, Gashan plays it over and over, as I sit nestled against the cold wall. The window to the chubby woman's home closes in a bang with a scream of rejection. He lifts the melody to the sky in a sort of message to the heavens for a relief of the aching heart. I place my fingers in my ears because the high pitches can't be tolerated. He's playing fingernails on a chalkboard then grabs the chalk to concoct a riddle of pain in front of my face. He's playing a riddle that I too well understand.

"Let me take you away from this, Rebecca. Remember? This was the reason that you called me."

"Why are you here, Gashan? How did you know that Anna would stop in this hamlet for the night?"

"I didn't know that she would stop here, at this crossing to my home. I did not know that the wealthy lords that I once played for, the noble who kicked me to the street once I lost my flute, would indeed step on me as they walked past me, a lonely, broken man on this street. I did not ask for this to happen. They acted as if they loved me just a few months ago, but without my flute, I am scum on the pond to them."

"Is this where you are from, Gashan?"

"No. I am from Ireland. But, I am trying to work for the shillings needed to board a boat and train to make it to the far side of Ireland. The flute's music enlivens my soul and keeps my family at peace. It also enlivens others and I make good money when I can play. Without my flute, all work is death. You understand this, don't you Rebecca?"

"Of course I understand this. But, to lie in the street because you lost your flute is fruitless."

"I thought I could make some more money before I crossed. But I am now aware that I must get back to my family. There is no money here to be had."

Something bizarre about these statements makes me glance at Gashan's flute. It is nearly ripped into two pieces, being held together by a sliver of wood in the center.

My realization shakes Gashan's nerves and he changes the conversation.

"This was my landlord's family who has taken in Anna. The lords own the money in Ireland, but they owe the British Kingdom large notes. Mr. Brown may not have what he needs to care for Anna when he returns. Lord Brown is gravely mistaken that his farm will feed his family, tenants and peasants over this next year. This is when Anna will really need you. The closer you come to her, the greater her courage will be to escape. I will go along to watch this family suffer for how they abandoned me," Gashan details, holding his flute up high which is now together in one piece.

"I don't want to see anyone suffer, Gashan! I came to love people, love Anna. We all are here to love each other. If they are going to suffer, we should assist them all! What kind of soul are you?"

"A lost soul, Rebecca. I am a soul who knows how to transform elements in life, how to transform darkness. I am a soul who looks into the darkness, recognizes that it is not real and transforms it. This is why you are so attracted to me. This is why you want me and need me, Rebecca!"

And with this realization, I drop my head back and look toward the stars, a slight green light dances through the darkness of what must be the north. That green light seems to reach into this passage, toward me, reminding me of the magic that can be collected in the darkness. *I don't want to live like this. I don't want to live like Anna or Gashan. I don't need to attract this pain. It's been shown to me many times that enlightened beings surround me. Sara, that lovely soul who approached me in my dreams. I miss journaling and getting responses from her. She lights my journey. She doesn't reach into darkness. She is a beacon of light. If I held her consciousness, I would be a beacon of light.*

Attachment to darkness. It is surrounding my life, but I don't have to participate. From the attachment, more darkness grows. I don't want to be with this man. I don't feel safe with Gashan. I am trapped. I have trapped myself within my longings until I'm lost for a way to escape.

Gashan lies back with his broken flute and I try to take my awareness away from him and into the trail of scent that has diminished. It is the same potato broth and pepper and vegetables that garnished my plate hundreds of times in my grandparent's 1800's home. That home was chipped on the outside but grew from love within its center.

Oh, the sweet scents of a loving childhood. The love in that house was as thick as molasses. You couldn't move anywhere without witnessing it. A tickle from my grandpa. Laughing tears from my grandmother's face as she tickles her husband back. Grandchildren running amok in the garden. Shoveling out of the ground an unknown person's big toe, as my grandpa called potatoes. Cooking rhubarb from a bitter abnormality into a sensual, sugary treat. Tea leaves, hot water, but no lemon. We didn't need lemon; Grandpa always planted the best mint tea leaves.

Oh, the love, the love. I've had it all along. It is who I am. There is no reason to separate myself. The pains occurred because I separated myself from that inner love.

CHAPTER 14

The Coming Dawn

My eyes open to the coming dawn. Its burnt orange halo barely caresses my view of the north horizon. Sweetness wafted away in the night. At least my heart is still. My eyes try to adjust to the stone walls enclosing this passage and to the space within the darkness.

The delusion of this place breaks my inner silence. The illusion of the dirt on which I sit makes me wonder if I'm not really here, if this may be more than a dream.

Ravens of three empty the space before me. Wings up then down. Beaks pecking in the dirt.

A dark scent stirs me. Smells of dirt mixed with sweat from my left thicken the air and protrude into my nostrils. My stillness is obstructed. This heavy smell is loathing, the misery of loneliness.

He is still here. Gashan lingers.

I now recognize this seductive, anguished man for who he is. A demon. My demon.

He is my longing. My loneliness. My Anguish.

For years, he has been calling me to my pain, to remember the darkness. He wants me to know his pain as well. Nevermore.

It is me who must break darkness. It is me who must emit the dancing inner lights.

There is light ahead and there is me. The halo expands without my action. I choose it and hope it chooses me. It creates the morning, erasing the dance of the Northern lights. Soon, it will break Gashan's sleep.

Living in misery means I've been lost. I forgot the spiritual essence of who I am. I know the first dimension of creating forward, as Sara has told me, and I must now practice it. I must relinquish that which does not sustain me. Every thought, acquaintance, and activity that whispers of doom must move on.

We must never name our demons.

Gashan sleeps, while I need not. Our breathing is not in rhythm. His hangs in despair while my breath mingles with hope. I shift my right shoulder toward the coming sun, hoping the left will glide free from the grip of his back.

In one moment, I get a break. He turns away from me. His heavy breath lifts his chin and settles his weight to the space opposite me. Unknowing, he grants my escape.

Rodents scurry beneath this ground from which I rise and dogs scavenge around the corner to my back. I must not awaken his form or his mind. I must sneak away quieter than I appeared. The animals don't still, snarling into possibly the last scraps of meat forever.

Silently, I tiptoe back down the passage toward the main street. I notice the dirt track beneath my bare feet. It is mixed with stone but is flat as an ironing board, long laid by peasants, the thousands who have walked this path. Some dust scatters as I take mental note of this place.

Anna's carriage is around the corner. I will be free, if I can remain silent between realms. I continue carefully while Gashan remains motionless. I pray that Gashan does not wake. Just a few more feet, and I will be around the corner. Please God, let me leave in silence. Please God, bring me to safety so I may find my way home. Sara, are you with me as I leave darkness?

No response. No Sara.

I pause when I see the man again sweeping his storefront and the gas lamp where Anna was handed over to the ladies. I pick up my feet to run at the hitched carriages, when a hound leaps in my path, tripping me, tossing me backward to the ground. As I hit the ground the dog's screech is my biggest concern, until I see Him awakening the passageway.

Gashan startles so abruptly that his feet and his moan echoes within the emptiness. He sees me.

I cannot jump in a carriage. Gashan cannot end up on Anna's journey. I head east, away from the gas lights, hugging the jagged walls that scrape my arm, and then south down a narrow channel to hopefully be guided out of sight.

My feeble energy allows me to run only so fast. I run, not looking back. I wonder if I possess an odor, a sound, or an essence that he can track. The path is easy to tread, but still my legs are weakening. Trees come into view, so I turn east again. The halo is now a reddish half-globe awakening the horizon before me, startling me into a fear of being seen.

Breathless, because my heart can't keep up with my reality, I run for what seems an eternity. Windows are thrown open even though clouds are gathering and mist is in the air. Steeples of red radiance, inverted and pointing to the earth, peek through the clouds and speckle the landscape ahead of me. I stop to ponder if I should throw myself into the woods. A band of light bares itself, extending toward me, as if to reach only me, identifying me. I look back. His bare feet and dingy pants are what I first notice, until he raises his hand high. Donning his flute high above his head, Gashan elicits a mighty stride. The darkness permeating from his eyes says he won't stop until he reaches his prey.

I catapult myself forward, tossing myself right and left through the thick brush and tall trees. The jolt puts me far enough ahead to be out his sight. I throw myself to the ground, nestle into its moistness and cover with brush. Emerald green earth. I taste the dew nestled on the leaves as I pack the earth loosely around my head.

The rain begins. Drizzling, in soft poetic dances with the leaves, becomes a song of surrender. I let go, although my chest is pounding, and just witness the chords playing in the air. What can he really do to me? Haunt me? Follow me? Follow Anna and haunt her? Break my spirit? Yes, that's it. He's been breaking my spirit all along. He will keep leading me to recall my pain.

I peer through my covering and see Gashan breaking the border of the row of stone. His flute, he holds safely away from his own needs to possess and destroy. The ravens do not budge from their position on a wooden lattice. A lady gathering vegetables from her small garden is not startled. He leaves no dust in his tracks. A mirage of my fear, he has been the point of my consciousness, my fears and my needs to understand pain. Nevermore.

He looks around in every direction, even to the sky. He turns to look back down the alley to see nothing but scatter. He turns again facing directly at me as the rain drops become larger, heavier, turning their song into a drumming meant to beat out the senses. Gashan lowers his head and takes two steps forward, listens. Despair comes over his face and tears rise from it. He drops to his knees, scattering the dust.

He is physical again. I know this not only from the dust but from the broken flute, now turned over onto itself with that sliver of wood connecting two halves, seared with jagged edges pointing to the sky.

What am I? Where am I? Leaves stick to my hair. I have to make it to Anna's carriage.

I capture all of my courage. I have to be brave. I no longer have the ability to find Anna within my mind. I can no longer sleep as Rebecca. I am embodied completely within this awareness of England, 1845.

As the woman now sees Gashan crying into the ground, she brings him scraps which sends the dogs to surround him, begging of him and jumping on him.

Quickly I rise from the ground and make the leap from the forest and towards Main Street where Anna and the carriages are hopefully still waiting. Sweating, panting, fearful, but willing, I lunge forward but am immediately spun around and knocked to the ground by a white stead. His eyes smile. This is what I see after my eyes are released from a dizzying spin, glaring through a covering to see his eyes say, "Don't live in this doom. Wake up."

The beauty backs off in a trot as show horses do. I feel grace, complete grace. Children of God answer each other's prayers.

I don't need to dust myself. My clothes did not contact this earth. I am now ready to end this journey through darkness.

I sprint due north, taking every alley that I know will lead me back to Anna. My thoughts are spinning. It was just a flute, not a knife, Rebecca. No one is attacking you with a knife anymore, Rebecca. It was a just a lousy, old, broken flute. An unconscious trigger of trauma so deeply buried yet painted on the canvas of my life.

I make it to the carriages quicker than expected, but am the last one to enter. I know her carriage. I can smell her scent of lilies, although it is diminishing. Sitting in the carriage with me is Mrs. Brown, Aaron, and Anna.

Within seconds, the team is off.

Anna no longer looks tearful; she looks like the devil herself. Her fine, brown hair is stretched in every direction. She massages then pulls at her forehead and the strands on top. Her face is ghostly white and the skin under her eyes droop in grays. Her pain is pure loss with no way to escape. Locked inside the stories of her mind, her face changes into an aged adult.

I place my hand on Anna's knee, close my eyes, and focus on a still heart. "We will get through this Anna."

The cursed lady across from us hands Anna parchment paper with scribbles of ink across its face. It lays on Anna's lap with the words "One Daughter's Love" on its face. I feel Anna's heat; her demon wants to unleash. She pushes the paper away, floating like a feather at first, but then landing on the dirty, wet floor. Beads of rain pound our carriage as the paper melts into brown. Anna disfigured a poem of love.

"Young lady, how dare you be so disrespectful!"

"Mother, she doesn't know what she's doing," Aaron answers.

"I am only trying to help this pitiful sight. Her mother said she's been writing poetry since she learned how to write. She should be thankful that I brought some of it for her," the lady says.

"I hear it is her God-given gift," Aaron responds.

"Well, a young woman should practice her gifts with devotion. It is invaluable to a man of esteem, should one ever take her as a wife," the lady says throwing her eyes upward. "Anna, you'll never find a husband with that look across your face. That pouting will turn away potential suitors. Don't you want to use your gift to provide entertainment to a home? Don't you want an admired home, Anna?"

You'll never find a husband, also told to me in a fit of anger by my mother.

Pause. Only silence.

"Answer me Anna!" the starched lady yells.

"Leave her be, mother." And with that, Aaron picks up the paper and folds it into a nothing of a tiny diminished square. He has a gentle smile toward what he is observing. He knows that Anna will get better. He understands that this is just a phase. His smile shows a silent wish to understand her better and a contemplation of how difficult she would be in marriage. She expects a lot, but not from the external world, from the soul.

"Aaron, you should not participate in these antics. She must comply so she will be a pleasant addition to our home, not a disturbance. Her father should have explained the trouble this young woman causes."

Aaron doesn't respond.

"Lord Kelly was hiding this all along. It's no wonder why he did not allow her to attend balls."

"Mother, I don't think that she wanted to be in attendance. I believe she has been grieving since her father died. We can be patient with her," Aaron explains tenderly, placing his hand on his mother's arm.

The pointed woman turns up her nose at Aaron's words, but she doesn't battle them either. She just turns her gaze to outside the carriage before retrieving her yarn and needle from the big black bag to knit.

Aaron reads, pretending to ignore the girl, but he can't ignore her. Every so often he gazes up to ponder how she became this way and how he can help her calm down and see that the road ahead is filled with opportunities. I know his thoughts because he speaks with his eyes and a tender smile that gently connects his humanness to her anguish. He holds the tiny square tightly.

Dried tears paint Anna's face and her stare is hollow.

I relax as everyone is in quiet nothingness.

The rain subsides and sunlight penetrates the small window to my left, casting my own shadow onto Anna's frail body.

A face appears through the light. It is vague and then structured into a middle-aged man. His arm reaches toward Anna and his hand holds a book, *The Prince*. As I concentrate more on the image an entire body appears, but the image turns to a 20-something man of infinite youth.

"Anna, you will always be my daughter. I am here. Choose happiness," the face says.

I turn to see Anna's response. A hand of golden light lies on her shoulder. This essence remains but no one sees or responds.

Suddenly, Anna's mouth begins to move, wanting to form words. She's relaxed one minute and heated the next.

"I don't want to be happy! How can I be happy when everyone I love has been ripped from my life," she screams.

Her face is scarlet red now and her pupils dilated. The sun continues to peak through the clouds outside, but inside our cabin thunder clouds are forming. A dense energy in the form of clouds settles in front of Anna. As she quickens her breathing and swells with anger, the clouds come together forming larger heads of delusion. As they move toward Anna's stomach they spin, become darker, moving one on top of the other until her space is pervaded by a tornadoing storm.

Anna bends over and holds her stomach in an obvious gesture of pain. Her father's face grows dimmer in the sun but the hand on her shoulder remains. The clouds overwhelm her senses, negating the love that she so yearns for. The clouds form a physical pain.

This moment doesn't pass. Anna doesn't want it to pass. She has a reason to be angry, a reason to call pain. She chooses it and allows it to choose her.

My heart stops racing about an hour into the trip and I am now completely able to focus on getting out of this darkness. I sense peace and know that both Anna and I will be lifted together. I now know how to accomplish this. I know to choose happiness. I won't expend my energy on worrying or asking 'why?' or 'why not?' The anguish appeared in my life because I lost a part of myself as a young adult, left the young shy girl with big dreams hidden under beliefs of mistrusting the world. I let life just take over; I let my circumstances take over instead of taking control myself. I drifted into any space that opened and attracted all that I knew. I knew distrust and abandonment. So, who would I attract in my life but men whom I could never trust and abandonment?

I'm done with that. We're getting out of this together, Anna and I. We are going to live lives of heavenly poetic justice, Anna with her poetry and the love of a husband, and I into an enlightened life. I will write my book, help others to be happy and enliven my soul. Any man, who comes into my life, will be of my choosing and he will want what I want, to live in sweetness of love, tasting the joy of life like molasses on my grandparent's table.

As my soul, my happiness, my belief in life start to expand, I can almost enjoy this trip that has become quite shaky, as the carriage is rattled by headwinds.

As night approaches and we are released from the carriage, waves crash on wood and scents of seaweed and muck are thick in the air.

Anna has calmed some and I help her take the hand of a gentleman who greets us. About as quickly as we are released from the carriage, we are shuffled into a door that opens from the main street. The sign above the door says "office", but inside the space looks like a home. There are four great rooms on the first floor and one is hosting a somewhat elegant spread of meats, cheese, potatoes and soup. It smells so delicious that I want a bite for myself.

Men talk business by the buffet while I follow the women into the kitchen. That is potato leek soup! I know the texture. I used to make it for my kids when they were younger. It's been so long since I really enjoyed cooking for my family. It became a chore these recent years.

I'm not given a bowl or a spoon, so I form a bowl with my hands and sip portions straight from the pot on the stove. As the bowl is formed in my mind, so to it is formed by my hands. It is beautiful, elegant, and heaven-like. The bowl is pewter. I like pewter. I can sip and taste the heavy potato broth with the delicacy of leaks intertwined. This is heaven.

I've experienced this before and so too has someone else who wrote the movie *What Dreams May Come*. Shortly after my dear friend Mazen died, I saw him in my lucid dreams. I went to see how my engineer friend, who loved his vodka more than life itself, was making out on the other side. What I saw was completely unexpected.

Mazen sat in a bar filled with other engineers. They were talking engineering, the exact topic that he loved when he was still alive. I asked Mazen why there wasn't a roof on the bar and he said, "It doesn't rain here, Rebecca. If we want it to rain, we'll create a roof." Then Mazen smiled, held out his empty hand. As soon as he cupped his hand a small shot-glass formed within it. Vodka appeared and he drank it with a smirky little smile.

"How did that happen?" I asked.

"If you think it exists, Rebecca, then it exists. We can still enjoy earthly pleasures here, if we so choose. What I think of, I call in. It appears and I can taste it. It is the same for you, just slower on your side."

When I awoke the next morning, a small pyramid that Mazen had given me a year prior to his death was no longer sitting in the center of my bookshelf. It was on the floor.

Later, when I watched the movie *What Dreams May Come* and saw Cuba Gooding Junior create a mug from his mind to drink coffee, God bumps covered my body. Someone else has also experienced this. I'd love to meet them someday.

After I take a few moments with the soup that has good memories for me, I place my attention back on Anna. She doesn't speak, as a matter-of-fact, she is not eating. She has not eaten all day. She is so numb and broken that her body cannot accept another thing thrown at it. It will reject food. I can see this in her jaw, her tense and hardened jaw. She is stopping nourishment from entering her body because she rejects the goodness. She would rather die than be without Dawson, be without love.

Beads of sweat mount on her brow after the women half force her into a few spoonfuls.

I expect the next episode to happen because I've come to this place myself once or twice before. Anna can't stand or make it to the sink; she just bows her head between her knees and hard-heaves onto the floor between her feet.

This will pass. It did for me.

The sky elicits a mellow roar this morning, making our trip over the water sway in some moments and still the next. The vessel is moving so very slowly.

Aaron is compelled to make Anna talk, but her jaw is clinched and her eyes hollow. The demon has left and nothing is occupying that inner shell. The cracking of thin skin is painful, so she remains numb.

I urge Aaron on to sit with her, to extend some human kindness that can provide a spark of aliveness. Her eyes and her body don't respond. But she doesn't pull away when he holds her hand. *Hopefully, she receives his hand fully.*

The water smacks the sides of our rusted-out vessel and the wind lifts it. Certainly, she can't deny this activity from beyond. I wonder what these sounds tell her, what they trigger in her memory. I wonder if there were storms on her journey from France to England after her father died. I marvel at the power of the water and wind and wonder if they trigger Anna. I wonder if the water and the wind are parts of Anna's story.

I must create my new story. I must make good triggers.

"My father was murdered," Anna blankly belches so that only Aaron can understand her words.

A murderous wave cracks the boat responding to her as if to say "yes, you are right Anna."

The trigger. The response. The confirmation. And we go deeper down the rabbit hole.

Anna's truth is a murdered father, a removal from security, a loveless home and now an extraction from love into the arms of strangers. She will paint this truth onto the canvas of her life if she holds onto this belief. Her elephant will paint her life and it will be all she sees, all she knows and all she believes. It will be her life again, and again and again.

And down she will tumble because it is like Anais Nin understood, great sensitives can't tolerate the slightest amount of suffering. Her shell of existence is her defense mechanism. To wither away, to deprive the body of nourishment is a defense against pain that may arise a million times before she accepts the fact that she created the pain.

Aaron has been reading her poetry for over an hour. He is now singing it into her ears. He is enlivened by the power of her words and the meanings he can't grasp.

One poem he keeps silent, and sneakily threads it to the bottom of the pile. In a brief moment he sits the papers to the side, and I am able to snatch it, the one so slyly hidden.

Through sweeping morning meadows of frostbitten blades
Serpent moves oh so gently, awaiting the inevitable illusion.

The knowledge of its power led.

I would gain but only a few breaths before it appeared
Bringing beams to burst across the Earth, as if to reach only me.

Strength moves beyond.

Inspiration overshadows as needs to create and to destroy pulverize
Inside of me.
But the melting brings nectar to the air and sweetness douses me
All the way below my calves.

Uncurling, tongue is tempted to taste both pleasure and pain
On the skin of divine grace.

She palters as I am lifted by a wave
Wishing the cattails had rhythm.

Release is destitute before arrival.

It is no wonder that he smirked at his first site of the words, Nectar, Release, Cattails.

With his stare becoming more encompassing, I wonder if he hasn't developed an attraction.

He gains his composure and sings one last poem of love into her ear.

"What was that fire in the light of our love
That consumed my heart and made me reach for God?

Stay here, my love. We have opened to a spring
And this enrapture is not yet formed.

Come back, my love. In your beauty
Is the moment the sun rises each morning.

I took a drink from the spring
of your soul granted to me.

My soul heard your world and lifted
Into the current that takes me."

Anna is unmoved. She has abandoned her own gift of love to try and find it in someone else.

Have I really forgotten that we are all connected? Every human, plant and animal, every sentient being is connected by life and by death. The connector never dies. The oxygen we breathe, the God we yearn to return to, we share. Our souls are a part of a grander soul. Every being that crosses our paths is a part of our grander soul.

When I return to my home, to my bed, to my beautiful children, I will remember this. I will be the soul that I came to earth to shine. I will no longer allow another person to diminish me.

Anna is diminishing. She's lost so much weight. Her ivory skin begins to hang from her cheeks and her wrists. She feels so small inside, so out of control of her destiny that she is allowing an external destiny, death, to take over.

If I could only teach her to expand into the love that Aaron offers, I could prove to her that in this love, she will find the strength to grow forward in life and find her partner again.

"Where is Dawson?" Anna finally mutters without change in her death eyes.

"He's in Derby, Anna. He is with your family at the abbey. It won't be long until he visits, I am certain" Aaron answers.

"I know," Anna sternly exclaims.

"If you imagine missing your brother over the days ahead, then you must love him and that's a good thing," Aaron says.

I walk across the boards and reach the bench upon which Anna sits, still clutching her poem in my hand. Grabbing hold of Anna's left I explain to her that she mustn't react from agony, not from the thoughts of what her mother has done.

"If you live in these thoughts that your mother ruined your life, separated and isolated you from love, you will embody this separation in your soul. But, if you act from the love in your heart, love will nourish you, finding its way closer to your life. You will create a loving world," I say out loud.

"I can't love," Anna whispers.

Did she just respond to Aaron or to me?

Anna is the mirror of my defenses, the walls I unknowingly built. So fearful of being hurt, so fearful of my lover's response, I not only hid from addressing the issues that stared me in the face, but I responded from these defenses by punishing.

Withdrawing love is a form of punishment. Creating jealousy and withdrawing love were my common punishments. Punishment and God do not co-habitate.

I take hold of the parchment and pen lying on Anna's lap. I have to write at this turning point. I cannot die like this, over angst in love.

My responses and my anger were always my indicators that my state of being was out-of-alignment. If I want trust, then I will trust. If I want love, then I will love. Everything else is just an illusion. Betrayal is an illusion. I shall make it small to a place of nothingness in my mind.

I lose grasp of the physical and the parchment leaves like a feather from my hands. Aaron reaches out, grabbing the paper and pen as they fall to the floor. He sees nothing but the indents etched by my mind.

Now I shall lay me down to sleep

I pray to the Lord my Soul to keep

As I love and play throughout the day

I pray the Lord is with me in every way

CHAPTER 15
Creating Forward

Rebecca is returning home, home to herself. She is awakening to the notion that it is her own gifts that she is running from. She is opening her eyes to the idea that Hugh and Paul appeared in her life to stir up every thought that kept her from experiencing her inner light. She is finally feeling that burst of insight as an awakening. Her relationships serve a purpose in her life; and yet, the ideas of betrayal and loss were created by a shadow in her life, a shadow created by her persona to mask the power of the little girl.

The persona must die. The illusion of separation must die and the truth will set her free. She knows that the book *A Return to Love* beautifully states how it is our Light and not our darkness in which we fear the most. Rebecca is closer to the truth, that if she were to focus on the sensitive gifts she had as a child that she may be so full of life that she will have no shadow. She is finding how to paint a grand picture in her life from the essence of her soul.

Rebecca will no longer pray from fear since she only wishes to create from love. She will look to the energies of the divine to create her life, a life born of gifts and love.

Perhaps Rebecca was not running from Paul. Perhaps she was

running from that essence inside in which she knew would be the death of her, the death of the one masking her true nature.

Rebecca is getting ready to no longer resist her deepest desires. Perhaps all else has been merely distractions.

•

CHAPTER 16
Lassaiz Faire

A cherubic face of porcelain greets us at the end of the plank, while water still pounds the vessel we are leaving. As a friend would, the young woman smiles kindly to Anna, stretching her arm forward in a greeting of acceptance. Splinters poke through my clothing and I am relieved to leave this steam boat. Anna is numb, but this allows her to be easily led by the arm.

"Anna, I'm glad you arrived safely. I am Elizabeth. I prepared a bed for you. I hope you will find it enjoyable during your stay. I believe we can be like sisters." Elizabeth's slender, green eyes match the color of her dress and complement the brown curls that fall down her back.

Anna returns a blank stare.

I take Anna's left arm to steady her as we make our way to a horse and buggy. The ride is short. We stop in front of a line of small stores. In the largest store front, a sign reads "NO IRISH NEED TO APPLY." Yet, we are in Ireland.

The bustling Brown's pull us into a large tavern with high wooden beams. A smoky mirror reflects a smudged outline of the bartender. This space is baked in darkness. Yet, British officials fill the space, merrily chatting, eating and drinking. Dishes of lamb and potatoes are thrown in every direction, even to Anna.

A fat man in britches raises his mug exclaiming, "The summer hunger is over! Ha! Our farms will be teaming with laborers once again!"

A few people cheer and others seem weary.

In solemnity, Mr. Brown listens thoroughly to the news ushered by the man to his right. I lean in closer, still holding onto Anna's arm. "The news is not good, Lord Brown. A dense fog settled from the north seas and killed much of the nearby potato crop. It's the wet rot again, I am afraid. The tenants are not paying their rents and landlords are abandoning their lands. Taxes are not getting paid, Mr. Brown. But, I'm sure this will clear up soon enough, as it always has. We'll do nothing and wait. We will let it take care of itself."

"Yes, I have heard. But I returned to Ireland for much more than these problems, dear Phillip. Evicting tenants is on my list. But, there is good news, Phillip. Our business is only set to expand. The demand for oat and barley is increasing in America. Furthermore, by the end of autumn, Aaron will be experienced in dividing our farm lands and working with the shipping companies in Cork. Taxes will be coming in and you and I can then focus on the Russians and the machines they want to grab from our mighty hands. They are paying high pounds."

My mind begins to race. I watch Anna only nibble at the potatoes. She doesn't want any meat. At least the potato has some vitamins. Her head hangs low as I am only beginning to awaken to this time period and the treachery that persisted into my own life.

I try to recall what I have learned about the period of the great potato famine. I don't remember how it began, why it continued or the amount of people who were left dead to rot and to be scowled by rodents and dogs. But I do recall that the Irish were some of the poorest people on the planet even before the famine, so the darkness was already here. I wonder where the compassion has gone in humans. How can millions of people be left without hope while others get wealthier from the land in which the hungry are left to die?

"Lassaiz Faire," Phillip responds raising his mug.

I nominally recall a quote I read in college. It was a sociologist who described Ireland as a nation of paupers. Before coming to Ireland the sociologist had witnessed wretchedness in all nations, as beggars on streets in towns of every nation. But never before stepping on the lands of Ireland had he witnessed an entire nation of paupers.

Lord Brown stands to give a quick farewell speech.

"I want to fill you with good news, as I am in the core of my own. We are in the midst of transformation, my friends. Idleness will no longer be the root of the people. Workhouses now house the poorest. The rebellions have diminished. Ships sail to America weekly with the fruits of our land and men are becoming laborers, on machines, in mills and in canals. This will be a prosperous land. And, to tell more of my good news, my son, Aaron, is set to be more prosperous than myself. He will be married in the spring, inheriting a silk empire in India."

The last statement infuriates me. Do these men own the women? Does a man get his wife's accomplishments? If a woman divorces, does she maintain her assets, her home, or her children? I know the answer is 'No.' I can see it in the eyes of the men and the demeanor of the women. This is the time of the Great Potato Famine. Is Anna headed into one of the greatest dooms known to human kind? My mind spurts out these thoughts like a knife spitting juice while slicing a hog. Thoughts of both saving Anna and feelings of despair cut into my soul. I don't know how to relax when there is such poverty in life and hunger in my soul.

Hunger. A feeling telling us to feed our souls.

I still my thoughts, remembering that I can't take every comment personally without getting caught in the web of darkness. If I listen to the information that infuriates me, I'll be split. If I keep asking 'why?' 'how?', I will turn myself against myself. I don't have to believe the history books, the ones written by the wealthy men. But I can believe in the power of the spirit of all. So now, in this moment, I begin. I recognize the higher consciousness of everyone here. Here is the only permanent strength. I'll take this strength to direct Anna. I can tell her to either fight for her love, or trust that she will have peace. Dilemma means either direction may hurt. And I remember Sara telling me that it is my choice to feel good or to feel bad. Fighting does not feel good. I will tell Anna to trust. I will tell Anna to eat while taking in the feeling of trust within her soul.

It is our duty to humankind to break free from the bonds of discord that we have created.

As we leave the village for a train, I walk as if I am Sara. A wide smile stretches across my face, although the taste of rotten skin seeps in from the damp air.

The air in the train is not much better. The Lord and his wife ramble on about Anna as if she is not even here. "If she continues like this, there will be no hope of meeting a suitor. Elizabeth is filled with glee and she fashions a few talents that the boys adore. I don't know of any talents bred in this girl Anna," the Lady says.

"Well, she will have to come around or face living in Cork forever, perhaps becoming a farm hand if she is not capable of anything else," the Lord replies.

"Anna, wake up!" I scream. "Do not listen to them. Do not live in such doom. Your life will turn around. Allow peace within until you witness your life changing for the better. Decide to be at peace with where you are at in this moment!"

The couple continues their utmost rudeness. "Her clothes are pitiful. The skin hangs on her bones. There's nothing there for a man to love."

I stand staring into Anna's face. "Anna, Anna! Wake up!" I slap her. Don't you see, Anna? You don't have to feel this way. Love is never separated. Your father and your brother love you. The distance does not matter. You will be with them both someday. Don't live in such doom!"

Her head shifts and for a moment she sits up straight. She blinks then looks directly into my eyes.

She finally sees me, if only for a second. "Stick up for yourself,

Anna. You're allowing others to choose how you feel. Wake up Anna! Scream if you must, scream Anna!"

And just like that, the loudest screech belts out of that skeleton girl's mouth. She keeps screaming and screaming this guttural urge, until the anger has control of her. Her mind and body lose control.

Mr. Brown leaps to her, placing his hand over her mouth while his wife holds Anna's hands down in fear of who she will harm. Anna wrestles against the couple, throwing the lady's arms away and biting into Mr. Brown's hand. The fight against her keepers seems to last forever. The fight lasts until Anna's fight is over.

Elizabeth sits still and does nothing. She feels she is a powerless actress in a dream.

Once Anna calms enough to make the Lady feel comfortable, Mrs. Brown addresses Elizabeth. "She cannot be seen with us. We cannot have our town thinking that we harbor a crazy person. Until she comes to her senses, you can deliver her food to your room. I will not have this in my home."

"Husband, I must send a telegram to Lord Kelly tomorrow. I will tell him that she is not fit to stay with us."

"It is much more complicated than that, my dear. We may have to give this a try for several months."

"Elizabeth, I know you don't want to be Anna's keeper, but you will have to be until she can act like a respectable part of our family."

Defeat. Complete defeat, like I have felt so many times. I meant only for her to disrupt her despair. I meant only for her to move her energy to get out of being locked-up. But, Anna let anger take hold. Anger will become a demon if you let him.

Anna has allowed the darkness to creep within. Recognizing that her mother killed her father, feeling abandoned and isolated from love, Anna sought relief from her wounds through Dawson. She felt abandoned and abandonment crept within. It created the exact circumstances to know itself. It created a longing that drove her to more longing. It created a life in the image of itself. Abandonment. And yet her mind believed that Dawson would heal her. And yet, it is not possible for another to heal the falseness that Anna owns. It is not possible for Paul to heal my longing.

Unconscious pain. It breathes in the mind of every human. The memories are stored within. We have separated ourselves from our Source and now feel powerless. In our powerless state the collective decides to take no action but instead to allow things to play out. These same humans then say that "everything happens for a reason."

Outside this train, in every scraggly body I see that unconscious pain. Men and women struggle to feed and clothe their children, while the children assume the duties of their parents by selling the shirts off their backs. Our belief that we are separated from love is the cause for poverty. True poverty is the condition of separation from our oneness. Our collective belief that we are powerless sustains the condition. The wounds of those who have taken power penetrate the little lives and their beliefs that the little are powerless are unleashed within the unsuspecting.

The solution is in our consciousness. The heart is the mind of the soul, through which feelings arise and give birth to thoughts. Those thoughts can quickly get twisted into unhealthy attitudes toward ourselves and others if we ignore the senses of the heart. The solution is to love the inner Self enough to realize that others' motivations are often out of fear. They too want love and search for it. They too make awful decisions out of pain. When we love ourselves totally, boundaries are clear, decisions wise and life is painted from peace. Inner love is the boundary that protects. For this little self knows that it changes and therefore, it is not real. The inner Self knows no harm and creates joy out of love, without concern of the changes to the little self.

How can I relay this to Anna? When can I get back to myself to do the same?

Anna's mind aches so her body feels bad; she is sick and then so becomes her thoughts. She gives up and her body lets go; her body is losing what it needs to heal, so her mind follows with it. Anna's accumulation of negative thoughts, starting with the death of her father and how she missed saying goodbye to him was one beginning of this wound.

I recall days that I forced comfort into my life. I'd force myself to lay by the pool and just read, observe and take in words that inspire me. I was trying to find happiness in words. I didn't realize at the time that I was awakening my own inspiration to write.

I stop day dreaming in realization of a way to reach Anna. Has Jane Austin been born yet? Does Northanger Abbey yet exist? I can't recall, but how I'd love to hand this novel to Anna right now. Reading Austin could create an attraction to Anna's inner love, her gift of poetry and that gift is filled with beauty. If she just read Jane Austin's words, she would create a field to recognize her true self and that field would never be lost.

I am starting to sense my truth. When I get back to my reality, I will re-write my story from love's point of view. I can no longer view my life from that of disappointment and despair, or my longings will get worse. The disappointment and despair took me farther from my soul, farther from my connection to the Source. And yet, the longing has always been a longing for the connection to Source.

My life actually changed for the better after Hugh. The separation made me feed my soul. It made me search deeper and deeper for my inner truth. And it made me so sick that I left my body during a diabetic attack and had an experience with Source that I would have otherwise not had experienced. It is this experience that I must share. The separation pulled me into choosing more education, a new job experience and adventure. That pull eventually led me to making much more money and then to taking my children to a place that would inspire them for life. Iceland. The separation from Paul is doing the same. It's changing my life for the better. When I return I choose to create something from my soul, from my journal.

"Where is Dawson? What have they done to him? What will they do to me?" Anna whispers slowly in sputtered words.

Waiting for the next painful event to happen is worse than remembering past pain. It shrivels the body from the soul. Angst separates the body and mind from the only source of true love and healing. Nervousness and glassy eyes are sure signs of not being present. Bad habits are only one of the many things that multiply when not centered in the body. Angst hinders liberation and stops the person from caring about their own person.

Angst is a powerful tool, and one owned by the land owners. Lassaiz Faire.

"Dawson is coming to save me; he must come to save me," Anna continues in her fear of abandonment from the one person who cares for her.

I compel Anna to shift one step further than her feelings. "Anna, your feelings will lead you out of this prison, but you are not your feelings! Your love for Dawson is greater than this despair. Feel your love for Dawson only and don't think of the future. Once you are at peace with that love in your heart, it will be time to act."

There must be action, but only once there is peace within. Gandhi.

I ponder the actions I can take to shift my own life toward happiness. I think of jumping off of my train, out of the corporate world and into what I love, spiritual teachings, writing and hiking the Colorado trails. And this exciting thought of following my heart leads my mind to poverty. *I would lose money. But, I'd be happy. Isolation. I would be far from my children. Yet, they'd have a beautiful place to visit. This feels so much better than staying in the corporate world. I can handle the lack of immediate cash. Even the worst I can handle.*

The people who fill the farmlands outside are multiplying, so I know we are in Cork. The train comes to a grinding halt on these tracks, at nowhere significant and in a place opposite abundance. I realize how far I've gone from my path and how desperate Anna must feel. We will continue to be amongst darkness if we don't let our own lights shine.

Smoke hangs obtrusively outside the windows. It is a dark, musty silence too hard to bear for a mind about to be awakened.

We may not be able to see our path ahead, yet we can assume the state of Grace. Jesus Christ.

Standing in this dim existence, I realize the source of my anxiety and sleepless nights. My subconscious was battered by a heaviness which is incongruent to who I am. My subconscious mind is inconsistent with the life that I want to live. I've been running from this awareness for a long time.

Only a bitter cold of sprinkling rain emerges through this fog. We walk into it and feel lost. But now faces appear and herald us off to get to the Lord's farm by sundown.

Once in the large farm house, the stairs remind me of my climb in life and so many dreams of either ascending stairs with barely enough breath to make them, or of descending the stairs rapidly to nothing but another climb back up. Up and down, up and down we go in life. But, to ascend and descend the same staircase for the entirety of adulthood must stop. I'm taking the train to a new destination. My train will not end here again.

The home is filled with smells of musk, and boiling vegetables and sweets. Elizabeth introduces her oldest sister and niece at the dinner table. They both joyfully respond in childlike curiosity of the newest guest while offering a seat and some bread.

After dinner, we are taken upstairs to a small triangular room. It is an attic modified for an unwelcomed guest. The silence is so deep that every whisper of this house can be heard. Elizabeth's niece is saying her prayers before bedtime.

"Now I lay me down to sleep. I pray the Lord my soul to keep. Thank you for another day. A chance to learn and a chance to play." I've never heard this prayer with these happy words before. It elicits joy instead of giving a fear of death. In my childhood, it was the Russians that could bomb us at night. And this is how I laid down to sleep most nights.

I lay on the cold hard floor beneath Anna and next to the window through which the wind creeps. Anna is asleep in the tiny cot above me wearing only a knit smock. I rise several times in the evening to cover her. Her newly found sister also sleeps in this pointed room at the top of two flights of stairs, but she is wearing warm evening clothes. Anna refused the gown that was offered her. The wood above us cracks and haws at the point in which the timbers meet. My mind falls silent as the harsh wind cracks into the pane of this tiny window. I shut my eyes in silence and dream of all of the food that just sat on the table before Anna, the food that went uneaten. The silky, white icing on the cake nudges a memory up into my consciousness. That same icing was in a dream that I had had soon after I met Paul. We sat in an apartment that was cluttered with dirty laundry. I licked silky, white icing from the top of a cake while Paul was on the phone telling someone that he was at work. He was lying. The door flew open and a woman walked in screaming "How could you do this to me?" She screamed and cried and screamed and cried some more. Paul panicked and tripped over his dirty laundry. I threw the cake at him with a pitch of a scream. I knew not else what to do. My subconscious mind knew his truth. Heaviness kept me from sleeping. Lack of sleep kept me from my power. Who has been painting my life?

A dance of our wounds, mine and Paul's, playing out on the canvas of our lives.

I bring my head to rest on Anna's shoulder. I whisper into her ear, "Fear not. Love is with you always. You feel betrayed now, but God never betrays you. You don't want to create your life in the awareness of betrayal, it will only lead to despair that has to be pruned from your existence. Even the smallest of candles shine in a dark room. We will find our inner lights together."

Lying prone on this hard floor, I imagine breathing into the chest of a man that I could love. Our breathing comes into sync and a melody of love takes over. A symphony plays in my heart. It rises as bliss and falls into a kiss. Distant from my love, another song plays. Loss. It is a melody of loss rising up from the living area downstairs. It beacons me with its painful fall to a deadening slowness.

I jump up and grab the doorknob that is already turning for me to make my leave and take to the spiral, wood staircase in a trepid yet rapid descent of knowing what I'll find. But, I have to see it. I have to face what I've created.

Dozens of backs face me, all dressed in black. There is weeping up front, especially from the lady who I believe to be Mrs. Brown. Anguish fills the air and it's difficult to move between the shoulders that are so tightly bound by despair. I move to the right of the room and gently slide within the wall of mourners. The flutist echoes the rain that pours into the fields outside, drowning out the earth, collecting within inverted mounds, vessels of mud. When the vessel no longer has the space to hold the rain, the earth overflows and rain flows to the next and then to the next opening. Anyone with an open mouth will take the sadness. The notes coming from the flute flows through me and I wallow in loss.

Mrs. Brown holds Elizabeth firmly in her heavy arms. But in this moment in time, Elizabeth is only about five years of age. Tears flow down both of their cheeks and Mr. Brown stands next to them, holding his face in his hands. Before them is a coffin, a tiny coffin of black wood with a porcelain face inside. The face is identical to that of Elizabeth. The crowd has been here for a while, as seen in their stained, and dried-up faces. There aren't many tears left, at least not for today. The flute plays their tears, acknowledging the pain of loss.

A parting occurs within the crowd, people move to corners, lean into walls and turn to no longer face the torment. Through this opening I see the flutist. His eyes are deeply painful and they lure me to the center of the torment.

"Mr. Gashan" Lord Brown speaks up, "you have paid your family's debts for a year. You did your best to save the twins from drowning. We will always be in your gratitude for saving Elizabeth. Your flute should be played to others with appreciation of its fineness. You may come with our family to Derby this summer. I know families who would honor this, even amongst an Irish Catholic. You can make extra money to tend to your family when you return. The offer is your choosing."

"Well, thank you Mr. Brown. I am just sorry that I could not save both of the children. My heart weeps for them," Gashan explains as his wife and children step toward him in their dirty farm clothes.

I recognize part of Gashan's suffering. Gashan, Mr. Brown's farmhand, has just saved the 5-year old Elizabeth from drowning but could not save her sister.

I bow my head to stare at the floor and hear no more talking and see no more bodies. I look up and his eyes make their way to mine. The crowd has vanished. All of them, gone in the darkness of the night tormenting rains.

"I would have had it all, Rebecca, if only the offer had been to take my wife and children with me to England. The lords didn't want to be seen in society with a bunch of paupers. They only agreed to dress me, not my family. And once I lost my flute, they no longer had need for me."

"What happened, Gashan?"

"The same that happened to you, Rebecca. Loss of love, loss of the instrument that brings joy. Loss of my instrument made my death."

"Are you reminding me of death, Gashan? You are trying to bring me into your despair?"

"Well, you haven't disagreed so far. Paul knew you have been in pain and it means that he is loved. You chose despair and it feeds him.

"The loss and betrayal turned to hate, Gashan. I fear that this is the real reason you brought me here, to participate in your hate. The actions from my hate split me into two. I am not returning to anger and hate."

"But, you have returned, Rebecca. You are here, participating in your liberation by facing those who hurt you. Turn your love to me and together we will be strong and conquer these feelings of loss. The story won't change. I lost my flute and I lost my family. You lost, well you lost….everything."

I feel like I'm living out a death wish. My habits reveal a death wish. And now I am stuck with a demon of pain. I relentlessly start crying in some sort of self-aggrandizement. I cry for the happiness that I lost, for the loss of my ability to be a completely strong mother and for those times that I came so close to God, those times that I clearly saw how important every soul is and how much God is a part of each and every one of us. I was so lucky to have these insights, these experiences. But, why don't they hold? Why couldn't I hold onto God's love through each moment of my life?

My own waling throws me to my knees, longing for the God that I once knew. I scream at the floor, I scream at Gashan. "You will not win! Your suffering will not beat me! Just because those in power sat back while your family withered and died does not mean I will lose to make you feel better. You cannot tell me that 'everything happens for a reason'! You want people to sit back and do nothing as if they were destitute in changing anything. You want their power! Before your tragedy, you were a pauper without anger. And now you don't let go of the struggle. You haunt people who have destitute imaginings so they will create sadness in their lives. You gain power from their emotions!"

I wale at the floor while screaming into my wounds. I scream inward pushing my face deeper into the floor. The yelling breaks through my wounds and now I remember. "I know the hunger! I remember, I remember! The hunger that we each have within ourselves turns us around." I cry. "Hunger turns us away from creations like you and pulls us to face the Source from which we came! I have been hungering for that connection that can't be found in humans. Hunger turns us toward our true power! This must be your greatest fear, Gashan!"

My tears dry as I truly see for the first time in a very long time. I stand and face Gashan. "I know from where you come, Gashan! I saw your kind in my near-death-experience years ago. I saw that you are powerless in the presence of love. My life was filled with writing and teaching spiritual practices and I was ready to write a book on my near-death-experience. I was ready to walk people into their power. That's when you showed up. I chose fear of financial loss and allowed you to step up. What would happen if I wrote a book that awoke people to the fact of their own power? What if I told people that you are from the astral world, the world that they call hell? What if I told them that they only need to self-love and have positive thoughts to cast you and all like you away? What if I told them that hell is not real, but a plane that is feeding off of them? You would lose your power! I stopped writing because of you! I've seen the truth Gashan!

"My hunger created diabetes, the kind that would allow me to see God. Once I did, the diabetes never returned. You must have known. You must have witnessed me fall to that floor knowing that my children would lose their mother if I didn't get to my kitchen for milk, or cheese, or peanut butter or anything that would stop my blood sugar from shooting out of control.

"Well Gashan, I did not make it to the kitchen. I fell in the hallway and I left my body. Those luminescent threads of golden-crimson lights that had been holding my body together untied. They unraveled from my feet and head, all the way to my navel. I left through my navel and headed toward the Light.

"But you could not have seen who was holding my arm. You could not have seen who had their hand on my heart! You do not live in such Light! You were not a part of my melting into my soul, while great beings kept my body alive. You could have not been near when a protector spirit carried me across human creations.

"I saw your many faces Gashan, all born out of fear and a lack of self-love. Creatures of all shapes and sizes. You are a creature and you cannot exist in love. Creatures dissolved in front of me as I realized my own power of love. And you stand ready to lose your power! You gave me all of my thoughts about Paul! Well, I love Paul and that is all that matters! I will always recognize you for who you are and will not carry your thoughts with me again. I will tell the world to stop focusing on the negative in any situation and to stop watching the news of stories of torrent. They have no idea who they are attracting."

I gently move into that space where I found Truth, that space that exists beyond the astral field so I may not only recall in my mind but exact this truth into my heart. I will bring this to Gashan and he will be no more. "I was so light after dissolving those useless, unreal demons. I was so light that I was able to reach a sphere on the outer edges of the universe. My protector spirit could not go with me, as he was an Earth protector. "And you Gashan cannot leave this Earth sphere because you feed off of human darkness."

"I went past every corner of creation, past every boundary of space and time. I saw that humanity was caught in unnecessary activity. I saw that they did not need tragedy to spur them forward. I saw their unnecessary thoughts lodged in your astral world. And I saw lights coming from those on earth who truly knew how to pray. In gratitude and oneness. I saw the prayer that keeps humanity alive. It is the grateful prayer of oneness. In this awe I completely expanded. I saw that all souls are stretched past space and time and that they are the Creator. I saw that when a human gives the oneness good thoughts in gratitude that the human gets the same back. But you Gashan, you wish that they believe they are mad and confused so you lie to them to keep them from their power!

"Nevermore Gashan! Nevermore!

"I saw the universe. I saw that everything in the universe exists inside of us as mere possibilities. Each a thought of God. The planets are within. They are not separate from us and are not distant. We are every possibility being born through each of us as unique expressions of our oneness. My soul has been wishing to be born and that was the true source of my longing. Longing just showed up as Paul. My hunger now turns me around, Gashan!.

"You could not have seen me then land on a sphere of brilliant white light before returning to my body lying on that floor. Every being who passed me on that sphere spoke to me with their minds. They have embodied love and live in a state of honor. They spoke to each other through their minds and all statements were of the purest intentions. Ill-will does not exist there and this is the state in which humanity is striving to become. Each individual on that sphere had one will, the will of the whole. Each individual's will was that of their own, but it never infringed upon someone else's will!

"And you Gashan, you are infringing upon the will of others by keeping them confused and in fear. This is how you feed and keep power in the wrong hands. On that sphere of brilliant light each being had their individual path and each path led to the betterment of the whole. You keep humans in a state of confusion so that they won't find their paths!" I scream.

Peace settles inside me. I have known this all along and yet I did not hold onto this connection. I do not know where my fear started. It could have been from a trauma, from a past life or inherited; yet, it does not matter from where fear comes. It matters where fear comes to rest. I will never again allow it to rest on me. My mind will feed the One.

"Gashan, that sphere had transcended suffering and perhaps you should begin doing the same. They do not intrude on the paths of others; and therefore, they are not intruded upon. You do the opposite. You make people believe that they are powerless and that everything happens for a reason. So, they do nothing. The little secret that you don't reveal is that when they have unnecessary thoughts, feelings and traumas, then the universe uses what was unnecessary to awaken them into something better. And these painful thoughts and feelings are unnecessary for them, but a buffet for you! Their hungers are always there to guide them higher and dilemmas give them the hunger to travel higher, and in this regard things happen for a reason. But the traumas are unnecessary and you know it!

"I choose to aim for an existence like that sphere where there is no suffering because there is no ill-will. They have transcended suffering by embodying love and I will learn to do the same."

And with that remembrance, my head smacks the air and the cold tears dry on my eyes. I turn away from my seducer. No more thoughts are required. I bolt up the stairs to make it to Anna's room, where I find Elizabeth with a tray of food and juice for both of them. I turn and shut the door, locking it boldly. Both girls jump when the door slams, thinking that a swift wind had carried up from downstairs, although I don't know how a wind could make it to this attic.

He can't get in. Gashan is locked out. I shudder watching the door knob turn left and right. I know who he is now and he can't get in. Oh God, don't let him get in. God's light is within me, God's light is within me I keep saying as a mantra over and over. And he can't because I won't let him in my life.

I throw my gaze at Anna, realizing that she is a shell of existence.

"This is cornbread, Anna. It is new to us. It doesn't taste great, but it's most of what we have right now. Father will bring oats today from his field. He is trying to find the farmhands now." Elizabeth says.

Anna takes one bite of the yellow muffin while her eyes gaze at the door handle in trepidation. She shakes as she watches the door handle turn left and right. Her arm reaches for something that is not here and her exhaustion lays her head back down in defeat.

"You must stop crying, Anna. It will make your body weak when it needs sustenance the most. You must stay strong so you can fulfill your purpose. If you want to love another, Anna, then love is your purpose. Stay strong to enjoy this someday," I beg of Anna.

CHAPTER 17
DEATH

Hours turned into days which turned into weeks. My life is lost to me. Time does not exist here inside of these walls.

Gashan can't enter the doorway, although he tries. Even in moments when Anna leaves the door wide open to head to the bath, Gashan just peers through hollow eyes into this death cell.

Anna hasn't been asked to help downstairs for days; the house is emptying, as is the farm land outside. Most immigrants, after witnessing these wooden frames of grief, left back to England, and the farm hands lay as corpses slightly below the damp earth outside.

Over the last three sunsets, Anna has only made it out of bed twice. Both times she dazedly made it to the chair that is propped by the tiny window. "Dawson, are you out there?" she wearily says, with the words broken as they leave her lips. Staring into nothing but death she tells him, "I am lost without you and I fear I haven't much time." And today, at her finale, she does not notice the man on his knees. Absent his flute, Gashan kneels in front of three tiny crosses made of sticks in front of the giant oak tree.

As always, her day is drawing to a close and she falls into bed. The same whispers leave her lips as she sleeps. "Dawson, are you there?" She doesn't stay in one position for long, the pain is too much. Her chin falls to her chest and she only has the energy to let out a couple of gasps that would normally create tears.

The skin on her face is pale, withdrawn and seems to be coalescing into the bed, into the whiteness of the sheets beneath her resting head. Cornmeal is her staple food, while the others get oats and wheat bread, and sometimes I have even smelled cabbage. But not today, the remainder of the family, Mr. and Mrs. Brown, Elizabeth and Aaron are packing hurriedly.

The same smock, now a dingy white, hangs from Anna's drastically altered limbs. Anna painfully leans over to rub her legs which are covered with reddish-blue spots. Elizabeth has all but abandoned Anna, assuming that she'll never have a sister, assuming that Anna is hopeless. She tried many times and ushered the help of several house maids to tend to Anna. They don't want Anna to be kept in this room. They wanted her to be a part of the dinners and gatherings in the city with Aaron and his companions, but they have to keep her here at the wish of the Lord.

It is the family's last evening and they are gathered together to sleep by the fireplace in the great room. Logs crackle and deep scents of hickory envelop me when I open the door, as if everything is right with the world.

The full Red Indian moon sits on the edge of the earth from outside this cracked window. My view of the moon is obstructed by Gashan's thin frame, bowing head and cupped hands that he holds high. I don't have to see his face; I don't have to hear his words. His body screams his screams. 'Why? Why? Why did you take them dear, God? Please bring them back to me!'

This event created the demon. His family, his wife, his children dead. "Why?" He asks God. Their youthful souls ripped from Earth. He realizes his own cowardice. He should have stood up to Lord Brown and demanded that his family travel with him to England. He should have demanded one set of clothing for each person, as the closets here overflow with fine clothing. His family did not have to look like paupers and a different set of events would have happened in England. His flute would not have broken. They would have stayed in England, not dependent upon the potatoes and he would not have returned to death.

Yet, his calling undermines his own asking. He calls out to something separate from himself. "Why God?" He would have found the courage from within. In the presence of oneness from within, attending to his own inner light, he would have carried his family to a different story. He is now firmly and consciously separated from himself. And in this moment, here in Ireland, the demon was born. The lights went out here and the lights went on, elsewhere.

Slight gasps from the bed turn me around to find Anna in a distressed state. Her mouth hangs open and her eyelids won't close. She's dehydrated so I call up my light, I call up this reality and use the luminescent threads that run between my being and this place. I grab the 2-day old glass of water that sits on the bed stand, cup Anna's neck with my arm, hold her head up toward my face and gently drip the water into her mouth. The water just runs down her cheeks. I try and try again, in the best state of calm that I can muster, but to no avail. My hand starts to tremble and I beg, just like Gashan, I beg Anna and I beg God. She is a light in life. She deserves to live. She has poetry of longing and loving to offer and a smile that would brighten the stormy nights and awaken those in an endless delusion.

My last attempt fails when fear catches me, faltering; I drop the glass to shatters on the floor. I hold her and just cry. She feels like a part of my self.

I mop the floor of the water with the gown that she refuses to wear and wipe her brow, again and again, holding to her life. Her frame has shrunk to make the bed big enough for two, so I lie next to her and hold onto her life. She is fevering.

"You grieve for what's beyond grief," I hear from beyond. "She doesn't die. No one dies," Rebecca. So, I do my best to stay strong for her to hold onto Anna.

Nestling beside her, I lay my head on her bony chest. The red sky glows in the corner of my eye across a haunted field. The waling is less outside than a week ago, as either the children are buried, the energy to cry has expended, or the waling ones have fallen over dead.

Hours pass and the moon is gone, leaving but a shimmering pink haze to light the corners of the room. The high beams overhead still creak to the sways of the wind and begin to reflect the gasping that is coming from Anna's chest.

I've only heard one beggar at the front door today. Lord Brown has the money and the means to give them the tools to fish. Instead, he gives them cornmeal and a meager helping of oats. All of the lambs have been slaughtered by now.

The smell of rotten blood catches my senses and I roll my eyes upward to find Anna's gums so swollen and bleeding. I do not know what to do other than hold onto her. Hopefully, she will feel my strength and feed herself back to a live being. I melt into her breathing, her disruptive breathing.

The smell of rotten blood soaks my core, first putrid and horrific, but then a sign of the life that was. The scent becomes a gentle connection between us and all of life. The scent turns to sweetness, to the life that has teamed through all of us; it lifts me in a sort of ecstasy within the connection of us all. The smell of thousands of violets within her blood bind me to a space of gratitude and I fall. I just fall into her being. I am completely helpless. The folds of her soul envelop me and it feels like silk folding my newborn skin. Golden lights merge us and I dance to her internal poetry.

I'm sitting on Papa's lap in the library. He loves this room. A dance of lavender plays outside the window, as far as the eye can reach. Papa always loves reading *The Prince* to me. I don't particularly care for it. But, I love sitting on his lap and I love it when he tickles me so hard that I fall to the hard floor, heaving in gasps of air, feeling completely alive in the knowing that we are happy.

Dawson, is that you? I miss you, Dawson. I long to have a hug from you. Are you near?

A few slow, shallow breaths.

Dawson. Oh, Dawson. I love you so. Why didn't you come for me before? You are my love and I needed you. I can't live without you. It is our love that kept me alive. It is our love that kept us strong when Mother killed Papa.

A dense air presses on the left side of my body. He is here, finally.

Dawson, the horrors of my life have been too much. It was only you who loved me. I want to love, just love, Dawson.

A warm hand gently lies on top of my left hand. It is sweet and kind and loving, a hand that tells me everything will be ok.

"Anna, I brought you a lily. You always loved yellow lilies."

Oh daddy, I have a chill. You know that I love the mountains, but not in the winter. Why did you bring us here again to these cold mountains?

"Cover with this blanket, dear."

My legs ache. They hurt so much that I don't' care if I'm sad. I need to get out of this snow.

"Here are more blankets. You can urinate in your clothes, it will warm your legs."

My nurse is angry in the library. She is yelling at daddy. He slaps her and tells her that he is trying to divorce mama. The nurse just has to wait until he can make a case for adultery against my mother. This is the only way in France.

The snow is freezing my toes, my ankles and my knees. They ache as I imagine dark rot down to my bones. My toes will need to be amputated.

I can't stand this snow any longer, papa.

My nurse leaves on horseback toward the south of France. Turning to face us in the kitchen, she shows her bitter face.

Momma is in anguish. Papa is ill in bed. "What did she do to you, husband? What did she do? Grace, please see that the kids make it to my sister's until their father gets better." Between screams and sobs of grief she is able to whisper, "I don't want them to have this suffering on their souls. It is best if they don't know what happened.

I am not angry at you for loving another woman. I don't want you to die."

I'm shuffled outside to the horses as momma lies crying on the floor next to papa's bed.

Dawson, oh Dawson, you have come. I see flowers everywhere because happiness has come to my heart.

Dawson nods in a gesture that says, "same to you, sister." He turns and sits at his desk to tend to his studies.

Who is this girl who is holding my hand, papa?

"Harriet, help Anna to see the Light, for I do not yet see it."

Harriet, do you know where they put my gown?

"You don't need a gown, Anna. You need to either breathe or not."

Gasping, searching for air, I stumble in and out of reality.

"Momma! Momma! It's Anna. I think she is dying. Come quick!" The words crack in a space that is distant, but calling and near.

I don't like the noises. I don't like the sound of the feet on the stairs.

"Dawson!"

"Anna, hang on. Bring her water, for her glass has spilled."

Harriet answers Elizabeth, *"Sister, water will only drown her and you will relive memories of my death. Allow her to be at peace and don't stir bad memories for yourself."*

The little Harriet moves closer with a sweet smile and a golden breath. I am in awe. I am happy but confused.

Elizabeth grabs my right hand and the pain it causes is obtrusively breaking. My bones shatter in the same cracks of the glass when it hit the floor.

I gasp to forget the pain, but it awakens. The shattered bones stop my breathing and then make my chest respond, first in a super-rapid stupidity like a fish out of water, and then at a loss for any gasps at all. Pain overwhelms, even the Anguish and Lucidity can't take over.

Gray clouds ease the pain but make it hard to see. They move me from discomfort. This is the space that I've come so many times before to just dream and float in my unease. I know these clouds intimately. They are my sadness and the place I come to cry.

I'm disoriented and wonder where the red moon settled. It is dusk, when I thought it was nearing sunrise. A blinding furry of the darkest clouds make it difficult to know which way to go.

Sounds echo behind the clouds, but I can't reach them. I imagine what is on the other side; it sounds like cries for love. Emeralds and diamonds of pure emotion are on the other side. The music plays in an attempt to reach the purest of emotions. First a flute in a sort of death march and then a piano playing a song that I remember, the wedding hymn.

The wedding. Mother. That song harkened that day, that day that mother wed. Mother. Lilies covered the gardens, but they were cut from their roots. The lilies I could have loved. I wish I would have touched the lilies.

Mother. Fists raised above her head, showing Lord Kelly what she is willing to do, even if it means the end of her marriage she sounds out from her being. "Bring Anna back now! I want my daughter here, in my home. I want my love with me now, or I will ensure the end of you!"

Love. What we won't do for love. *But, I am here Mamma. You shouldn't hurt your life for love of what will always be. I am here, always.*

And then lying on the floor of the library, in anguish. Holding to letters that she had discovered after the death of Papa, letters between him and his lover, my nurse. Lord Kelly holds her. He is the only one to comfort her and the only one to help her during mourning, during healing.

She was still in healing in Derby. The hundred days fly past me in my little well of existence. Mamma didn't make any decisions. She was hurting too much to notice us, to tend to me and Dawson. Her hurt was deep. She didn't imagine me here, existing elsewhere.

"Daughter, just look them in the eyes and they will faint. Daughter, just look at the faces in the clouds and they will fail to exist."

I am alone in this cloud with nowhere in sight. Voices within the clouds reach me. "Anna, there is lamb stew right over here. Anna, Dawson is waiting for you by your bed."

I try to grasp reality with the thickening of my blood and the breaks in my knees. But, the sun has long set and only darkness hangs between the obtrusive clouds.

Harriet's hand remains on mine and her smile doesn't change. There is nothing to fear her eyes tell me.

I'm carried with the dense cloud as it descends closer to the earth. The mist swirls and vague shapes begin taking the form of disturbed faces. A snake and then a mask appear and disappear. I'm drawn deeper into the dark mist when a reptile that I have never seen before faces me directly, eye to eye and then chomps his jaws toward my being.

Nothing to fear, Anna.

A wicked, red glow penetrates the space from his eyes. The center of his eyes swirl in a sort of hypnotizing dance. He's confused, daunted by life without means to be anything more than this scaly creature of instinct.

A recognizing smile appears on my lips. *I see. Now I see. You are embedded in every living creature, in humans, animals, rodents, birds and reptiles.*

He swipes his tail around from his back and lunges it in my direction, in an attempt to grab me.

As my vision becomes clearer, I become clearer. *I used guilt and jealousy to have love in my life. Dawson honored my pleas to not hurt me. I used my pain, putting fear in him that I would die without him, to keep him close to me. I see you, monster. I see you. He loved me without my need to hurt him, without my need to put fear in him. My own fears hurt us both. I see you!*

I am loved and I don't need you. I am more than a person who scares others to love them. I am love.

I am still. The hold between our eyes won't leave.

I melt and I surrender. *This is not I. I was just human. I was in delusion. But you, you are done.*

Vanquished. Melting into himself. He can't look into the eyes of a bigger soul. Violet vapor engulfs my little self.

I don't have to keep going, I can go back. I gasp and am aware that there are several people in the room, but this awareness is only for a moment.

This dense cloud, holding within the moisture of my overwhelming emotions kept me from seeing in life. I chose this cloud; and now I choose to set it free.

A slight lift begins as I release my fear and let go of the pain that enraptures my knees.

Mon Pere!

Comfort comes from all spaces. Everything that I ever was and ever will be, I now know. It's my choice.

Papa, hold me!

The birds in my backyard are present. They are inside of my soul. An emerald green gown appears and then a woman moves into it. It reaches the spans of the universe. It thickens as I put my awareness on it. The beauty is overwhelming. I want to touch her, to be like her, but I can't reach her. Her limbs thicken and it temps me more to understand her. I can only imagine the green gowns. I wait for my chance, for my choice to live in this beauty. Venus.

Chanting pervades the space in which I move. *Halleluiah…..Om……. Hum.*

It's so beautiful! I see the sounds! I want it. A multitude of voices surround me. You are Light and put yourselves on the hill to show your Light to others.

Words, symbols, letters rise from those who are calling from Earth. Heads tiered in bronze lips, still, yet wrapping their arms around the multitudes. Egg-shaped lights hanging on Dawson's heals. I will know these heads of light. H...then a white cloud through which I choose to see...I was just trying to understand love...it was an internal mission...love. V....Y...there is more here, but how can I accept it all?...V

Choruses sing in mesmerizing tones hitting high notes asking for forgiveness. Chants have been here forever. Chants reach into the crevices and plant gratitude for knowing this space, while still being human. Monks sing in a space that I want of.

I am no longer disoriented. I know exactly where I am going. I am floating, but it feels like being expanded. The best of the earth, the love, prayers, compassion, singing birds, tuning harps, birthing mothers, families welcoming their soldier home, families sharing food at a dinner table and babies laughing all sing in my soul.

The clouds lighten into a white mist, surrounding me. A hand reaches through the cloud to my right.

It's my brother. It's Phil! He pulls me into a field of flowers. For a moment, the length I don't know, we pause. It is light here and I am calm.

Harriet appears to tell me that with what I learned about love as Anna, I will take to help birthing mothers from this side of existence. Harriet explains that with the light that I give to these birthing mothers will ensure that I have great relationships with my own children someday.

Mothers take on the pain of the world. Mothers envelop the hurts of their children, their husbands, their neighbors, their bosses, the lost in the world, the helpless, the hopeful, the grief-stricken, the homeless, the rejected and then end up rejected.

In the corner is my mother. Weeping. She's weeping over the loss of her first child, the stillborn child. She is pregnant with me, with Rebecca. She can't handle the loss. She doesn't know how she can be strong for her second baby, for me. She is not aware that her emotions are being placed within me.

The clouds ascend in a moist, dense duty of relinquishment.

They take me into their core and I am again disoriented, lost in the mist of life, trying to recognize who I really am.

Finally, dawn breaks. The sun is rising over this Deep South French town. I run to catch it. I'm not good with my feet, yet I make it up the hill from the Cane River. I make it to my grandpa, standing on the top of the small mound of dirt, with a smile in my heart. I've made it. I am Rebecca and I have another chance.

CHAPTER 18
MOTHER

"Mom! Mom!"

"Come on, Mom. Wake up. It's Jacob and Marisha."

It's hot in here. I'm drained. Can't move.

"What's wrong? Are you sick? Talk to us Mom." I now recognize Marisha's voice.

I roll to my back and roll back my eyes before opening the lids. The faces of my loves, my babies, stare blankly and frightfully into my face. How could I let them see me like this? Oh, my dear, sweet children.

"I'm not feeling well. But I'll be ok," I barely mutter.

"Do you need to go to the hospital?" Jacob asks.

"No son."

"Do you need medicine?" He looks so frightened.

This awful internal illness is exactly what I never wanted to pass to my children.

"Aspirin will help. There is some right inside the door of the bathroom," I explain so he feels he can help me.

"We were so worried this weekend at dad's when you never answered your phone. We couldn't go to school this morning until we knew that you were ok," Marisha says with her eyes in the shape of tear drops.

I hear the faucet running and know that Jacob is getting me water, which is much needed because the hot sweats across my skin tell me that I'm dehydrated.

"Don't go to work today mom. Get better first."

"I won't Marisha. You are so right, my dear daughter."

I drink the water although it's difficult to swallow and I chew on the aspirin. I allow my children to pull me up by the arms and lead me to my bed.

I should be tucking them in. It shouldn't be the other way around when their mother isn't really sick. I am really sick. It's just not a sickness lab technicians will detect in their little petri dishes.

My kids spend an hour by my bed listening to my bullshit about eating something bad that led me to puking in the bathroom, which of course is how I ended up lying outside the bathroom door.

"I feel much better now, especially after the water. Thanks Jacob."

I call into work with the same story. "I am so ill that this will take a few days for recovery." And so it will. This is a deep sadness that I must digest and put away for eternity.

I convince my children that I will be fine. But as they turn to drive off to school, Jacob has a pill that will help my disease. A happy pill.

"Guess what, mom? I got my acceptance letter to college on Saturday!"

Now this is the right kind of medicine for my illness.

He leans over so I can give him a big hug. I give Marisha a deserving kiss on the cheek and a wink before they set off for their day. I am set to close this wound.

Once I hear the door lock behind them, I know I have to get any sort of rejuvenation possible. I feel drugged and beaten. But the realization of how many wounds I've taken on sinks me into this bed. The mother feels that she must take on everyone's pain, that she must be helpers to all. She feels responsible for everyone else's happiness. The mother inside of us absorbs other's fears and sorrows, takes the pain for the sake of the happiness of others. *I'm glad it's me who's in this bed suffering and not my kids.*

A hot shower calls me. The cleansing is desperately needed. My body must waken itself. The shower is where I wash my wounds and clear my mind.

As I lean my head back to let the water pour over my head and down my face and back, I see her in my mind's eye. I see Anna perishing. Her wounds were visible in the end. Visible as the bones that protruded through her rough flesh and the sores on her skin. The internal pain was a physical blow and then this pain unleashed itself into physical reality.

I turn the heat up on the water, as hot as I can take it. I want it to wash away my pain, cleanse the loss that is held in my cells.

Anna would not have met her demise had she loved herself first. She was never taught the importance of self-love. Are any of us?

I recall a Sudanese taxi driver in Chicago who once told me that I was worth 12 camels. He had a big smile on his face and said that my personality brightened up his car. "Your husband sure is lucky!" So, I guess 12 camels are quite valuable. I can't equate my worth to anything in my world. I trade my love, my heart and my joy to share the same with others. That value is priceless, yet I've never lived in that knowing. I know how important it is now. I wonder why it's not a value that society teaches children.

My sense of self-worth expired when I got weak and I got weak because I put energy into false attachments. I've taken my own lack of self-love out to others in hopes they will fill that void. Their love cannot fill my void. Asking 'Why?' only separated me from the moment, from the possibilities of the moment and from my own soul. I can love right now. I will be fine. *No, I am fine!*

I take a few deep breaths, soaking up the stings from the water on my back. My full awareness flows into my body and I realize that its tiredness has been showing my pain for far too long.

Once in the kitchen, holding onto my coffee which is quickly getting cold, I stare at my journal lying on the table. I need to fight for myself and describe this fight in my journal because it is the Good Fight. It is the one that I can begin to understand now, as the mind must align to all there is. We are all connected. We are all the God in which we are searching.

I turn to a page in my journal from a year ago:

If I don't allow negativity around me then he can't hurt me. It hurts me when he doesn't return my calls. It doesn't make sense. He can't be that busy. I don't like the way he ignores the question. It's like he's hiding something. This doesn't feel right. But, I could lose the love of my life if I let him go. I need to stop asking why and stop looking at the problems. I should start looking at the solutions and the way forward. Nurture yourself; nurture the essence of who you really are. Say you're a motivational speaker and that you are in love with life. The right words will come.

I'm afraid of breaking up. Our love has inspired me. I'm afraid of how he'll react and I am afraid of hurting him. The 'blowing up' will come next if I don't manage my thoughts. Hurting Paul is a big part of my negative thoughts; he's done nothing to me. Our goals are the same, to feel good. But, if building a relationship together is his goal, he would be addressing my concerns, addressing my heart. He is not. Rebecca, you are letting someone else's problems, his hang-ups, bring you down. There is no conflict, either we have the same goal or we don't. I'm not in a trusting relationship. It feels devaluing. I don't like wasting my energy on this.

I close the journal and stare out the window knowing that I have much to digest. And only then can I become my own Truth. I'm not certain where I was just at, in that attic, in that bed by the window through which the cold swept. I was in the midst of dying of a broken heart. But where did it start? In Anna's mind? She believed in the love of her perfect father and the treachery of a murderous mother. Yet, her mother didn't kill her father. His mistress killed him. Her mother was still in mourning during their short time in England. She probably didn't have the strength to deal with more heart ache. She probably was left with guilt beyond imagination upon learning of the loss of Anna. The loss of her daughter, who she had not been actively loving.

My own mother's grief comes into view and her aching heart. Loss can be unconsciously passed on, inherited. Loss can travel from the blood of the mother to the blood of the unborn child. My loss of love has occurred because I believed in loss.

I re-open my journal and begin to write my future.

Love has always been my destiny. It seems to have been born of me. I am not separate from my soul mate; we are finding each other. Nefertiti has been my symbol of separation of love, but now let her be my symbol of love ever-after. This is the kind of heart that doesn't die no matter how far two people are apart, dead or alive.

I was sacrificing the long term for short term benefits. I must think long term, about a lasting relationship and how to create that. It won't happen if I keep feeling resentful after giving my love. Eternal heart-love feels better than passionate attachments. Building upon love feels better than biding time. I created nothing but turmoil with Paul. Today begins my creation of happiness.

My lack of self-worth and distrust went hand-in-hand. I believed life would throw me lemons, and so it did. Gashan kept me there as I drove to understand the loss and the pain, as I kept looking back.

Today I choose the mind-set of Sara. A peaceful mindset, choosing only the good things in life. I am willing to give up good for the great.

I am putting my attention on the good things in life. From this, the good will expand. I will attract only goodness. Oneness is all that is real; the rest, an illusion.

I used to deflect love by not addressing the issues. I'd wall myself from potential pain. My subconscious was actually focusing on loss, and loss I attracted. Perhaps we never had to create this loss.

I've often wished that I would be like others who aren't so attracted to being in love. Some are attracted to connecting with lots of people, to being a part of a community. Others are inspired by accumulating wealth. And still others are attracted to relationships, yet unlike myself, create brilliantly happy lives with an abundance of love in their families that withstands hardships. My inner love must now flower. It has a message that I will find.

I pause and lift my pen away from the journal. A nudging emotional pain floats into my awareness and I remember that God is benevolent but realize, Creation, not so much.

And this is the beginning of my book, *Creating Forward*.

What is creation? A happy state? A baby? Career? A new home? A lifestyle? I will learn to create happiness.

This reminds me of reminders from last winter. First, I was in a high school classroom judging a debate and was fortunate enough to hear a slew of misguided cases from the students. The issue was the government funding of fuel-efficient cars. Instead of arguing the argument, one student countered the opponent's use of the word 'efficiency' with the idea that Webster's Dictionary is not valid. The worthless argument that ensued sucked them further off-topic to never return.

But, I did think on this afterwards. The interpretation of each word would be different depending on the experiences of the individual. The created will describe himself and his creator differently than the Creator's definition. Defining ourselves and living within a definition is finality. Seeing myself as created, I would express my life from the stand point of completion. But talking as a creator, I seek to attract the abundance of the universe. The dance is my creation. We must grow, create and expand.

Second, I left the students for lunch. My mind was on the most recent break-up with Paul. I was in despair over ending it and not ending it sooner. Right there, on a 12-foot banner hanging from the ceiling, was the message. "Stop participating in what doesn't feel good." I had to go back to high school to get the reminder.

I leaf through my journal to that President's Day weekend to find my state of mind. And there it is:

But what if that which doesn't make me feel good pushes me on to what does?

"Just because I'm hurting doesn't mean I'm hurt." - Coldplay

And what did I choose, but to go back to him and trust him again? The love felt good, that's why I went.

But, it wasn't love; it was pain that I felt. I was drawn to pain. How did my knowing of living from the heart escape me? The law of grace, the fourth principle, expands the consciousness through truth and from that space, I cannot be stricken. My life becomes balanced and I would live beyond discord and only attract grace. This will take some work, some mental shifts and releasing to get me there, but I'm finally willing and ready.

Instead of wanting love, I am love.

Love cannot be found outside of me. Joy does not breathe separately from me. Peace is not a staple bought at the candy store. I write in my journal: *I am love, joy and peace in compassion. Now I must embody this principle*

It's Wednesday and I make it back to work, but wish I weren't here. It's definitely time for a vacation and this is the only place my mind lives today. I want to take three weeks away from work. I want to go to a spiritual place, a space of healing.

I don't think these lungs could handle 14,000 feet at Machu Picchu. But, it would be my first pick. I can return to Colorado. It is my favorite place in the world, so why not? But then, I could also step outside of my comfort zone, break a few barriers and allow myself to go to a place that I've always wanted to experience for myself.

After lunch I take a coffee in a lonely break room. As it's percolating I stare out the tiny window and watch the clouds gather. I see this scene so often. I sit in this empty room, even when it's filled with co-workers; stare out the window in hopes that I'll leave this place someday soon.

If you could go any place in the world, where would you go, Rebecca? Bali, I'd go to Bali.

And just like that, it is settled. The plane and the hotel room are booked this very evening. I'll be leaving in exactly two months.

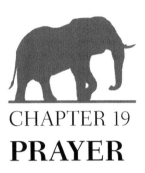

CHAPTER 19
PRAYER

Luckily I find a tiny tourist book on Bali in the San Francisco airport. It's all I have to lead me, other than my memories of reading 'Love', the last section in *Eat Pray Love*. I luck out on the second leg of my flight with two empty seats next to me. I stuff the little dark blue pillow into the window, gather my legs up onto the seats and cover with a blanket. I can actually sleep on this twelve hour journey to South Korea.

After barely finding my way to the final leg of my trip to Indonesia, it is nearing nightfall and I wonder how it will be to arrive alone in the dark of a strange place.

I soon find out, as the excitement that built over the last seven hours mirrors the racing of my heart upon arrival. Full of hope, I enjoyed the plane food and even the little plastic utensils, I laughed at the movie that I didn't watch, held my pee in worry that I'd miss something out the window and relished the white, not-so-fluffy, slippers that kept only a portion of my feet warm. This was the quickest seven hour flight of my life.

Of course, I jump into the wrong waiting line to be asked 30-minutes later for the visa that I should have picked up at the first window. The guy is a little disappointed in me, but he sees the anticipation in my eyes and calls someone over to issue me a visa, holding up others who are anxious as I to break through. He doesn't even ask for my final destination.

Yep, it's dark. It is 1:30am. It's not difficult to find my way out of this small airport. The crowd is pushing in only one direction. A herd of hosts hold signs in the dark. I scan the nearly fifty white cards that are pleasingly held up between the cracks in the crowd. I scan right to left and then left to right. I call the names 'Conrad' and 'Rebecca'. No response. I go to the far end of the building to view empty cars and return to a now smaller crowd of drivers. I don't see a single card with either 'Rebecca' or 'Murphy' written on it. Of course, many of the cards are written in Balinese. I guess it's Balinese. Damn, I don't even know what language they speak.

A man notices my dismay and I explain that the Conrad is supposed to pick me up.

"They aren't here. It's too late for them to pick you up."

"But, they didn't complain when I gave them my arrival time. They said they would be here" I explain.

With a huge smile the man grabs my luggage and says, "It's too late for them. Come with me."

He hurriedly ushers me through a parking lot and a worry sets in. I don't know this man. Where are we going?

The trunk of a taxi cab creaks as he opens it. I wonder if it will fall apart when he slams it shut. He just as anxiously opens my door and tells me to get in. Without thinking, I do as he says.

Now I feel fear. It is very dark outside. No lighting. Why is he driving so fast? Where is he taking me?

"What is your name?" he asks.

"Rebecca. I am from Canada," I say in hopes that he hates the Canadians less than he hates Americans, because he could be a terrorist.

"Where are you going?"

"To the Conrad in Nusa Dua" I answer.

"The hotel? The Conrad?"

"Yes. The Conrad hotel in Nusa Dua," I answer again.

"Ok. The Tajuathingy Benoa Conrad," is what I hear him say. "We go to the hotel now," he says.

"What is the Benoa?" I ask.

"Only one Conrad in Bali. No Conrad in Nusa Dua. I take you to the Tajuathingy Benoa Conrad."

"Oh. Ok. I didn't look closely at the address before I left." Damn. I really thought it was in Nusa Dua. That's the name I remember.

He takes the winding, narrow streets too fast for my liking. My mind begins to race. Why is he in such a hurry? It's so dark. I see a few dark images line the streets beneath palm trees. Why are people out this late at night with nothing but dark streets to inhabit? I notice bending slabs of wood that must be the slums.

He takes me through a traffic circle with an actual light in the center. There's a statue of a man, a chariot and three horses. It's like the one in Berlin, and Paris and Rome for that matter. But the streets darken again and are obviously much narrower because palm trees are scraping the taxi. Even if it wasn't dark, my view would be lost for the bark edging closer to my face.

I'm scared to crack my window like the driver's. Odd scents enter the cab, scents to which I'm not accustomed. Excretion, maybe with a hint of curry and other spices I haven't tasted. This is my first taste of these dark spices. I notice a hint of yet another perfume. It's familiar. It's a familiar incense.

A tall lean man walks in the center of the street, straight toward our taxi. The driver doesn't slow down, only hugs the palm trees more.

"A man, in the street, at this hour?" I ask. I can see the outlines of bent-over huts, broken walkways and dogs scavenging within the cracks. This is complete poverty. My hotel cannot be near these raucous slums and I know my hotel wasn't this far from the airport. How long have we been driving?

My fears are almost peaked when we turn right into a paved driveway with a hut filled with uniformed men. The fear burns like a hot iron in my stomach and ascends in a fury when a man sticks a flashlight into my face. Another is opening the trunk and yet another is pushing a long shiny object underneath our car.

The one with the flashlight motions for me to roll down my window. Shaking, I can't find the button. It's a turn handle. My sweaty hand rolls the window down two turns.

"Just checking for your safety, madam. No bombs." And, they all smile and wave with their outstretched hands almost reaching into my seat. "Peace to you. Have a beautiful stay in Bali!"

And like that, the car is whisked up a hill by the speedy driver. When the car comes to a halt, all I see is the most brilliant lobby that I could image. Immaculate open space with hints of dancing lights reflecting off of marble that holds a myriad of flower statues as tall as the Eiffel Tower.

The driver opens my door. He carries my luggage and the biggest smile imaginable. "Did I get you here quick enough? You should have plenty of rest so you can enjoy your day in Bali tomorrow. Get good rest. Good rest is good for the soul."

I tip him big. I mean, I really tip him big.

I can't sleep. This place is too beautiful. The people are overwhelmingly welcoming and peaceful and happy. I sit on my balcony with my legs dangling into the swimming pool that meanders from the beach into my room and I start my day at 2:30am by awaiting the rising sun over the Bali Sea.

"Ketut Liyer. Do you know him?" I ask the receptionist.

"Oh yes," she says with a smile. "He is in Ms. Gilbert's book. Any taxi driver can take you to his home."

"Do I need an appointment?"

"No. Just arrive early. He's been very busy since the book."

It's 6:00am. So I am good.

"How far is it to Ketut's home?" I ask the taxi driver after breakfast.

"Not far. Only 40 kilometers."

"Great!" I'm happy that I can be there by 8:00 am.

After dodging bikes, taxis, dogs, babies driving motor scooters, and pedestrians on this major highway, we make it. It's 10:00am.

I get number 19 on one of those little cards like you might find at the driver's license bureau. Ketut can only see 25 people a day. A few more motor scooters and I would have missed my chance. Next time, I'm leaving before sun-up.

I wasn't going to come all of the way to Bali and miss seeing the healer that Elizabeth Gilbert made internationally famous. Plus, I need the advice. I want to start and end this vacation happier than I arrived.

I sit within the garden that is his home. On a small stoop outside a line of bedrooms, I am settled. This moment is like a prayer. I am completely still inside. The silence is vast. Ketut is with person number seven, so I have all day to ponder. But, pondering is not what I do. This place is not of the mind; it is of the soul.

I sit in what feels like gratitude. It's not pouring out of me and it's not entering. It just is. I have no place to run to. Nothing to fear. I am not in a hurry. Complete peace and faith dwell within me as I know number 19 will be called and in the hours prior to that time, I can just experience the moment. Anxiety doesn't exist.

Nothing can distract me from the inner prayer because all I witness is God's beauty. There's no one to call. Jacob is at baseball camp and Marisha is in Italy without a global phone. Isn't that funny? Marisha is living 'Eat' and I'm living 'Love' at the same moment. I realize that she's been there about 24 hours more than I've been here, although we left at the same time.

A text comes through my phone. "Marisha has food poisoning and is in a hospital in Rome."

I close my eyes, connect to my daughter's soul and send the healing energy that I have captured in this space. I notice that I worry about her, but I remain the observer of this thought. After thirty minutes, I feel we can both relax and decide to wonder amongst the beauty. (It won't be another three weeks until I learn of the hours that Marisha lay on that cold hospital floor in agony while an IV drip kept her from dehydration.)

There is nothing to do here but love. I love the birds and I don't just mean the ones singing in the trees. I love the birds that are laughing at me from within the large cages. The toucan-looking bird laughs the hardest. He can tell that his large beak makes me jump back so he throws his head around and around as if it's sitting on a spring. He then throws his whole body forward, lodging his nose in the inch-wide crack. He shakes his shoulders a little as if he's letting out a big giggle and then says "Tat tat". And what, I thought he was going to speak English?

The celestial blue bird with the fanned head rolls her ruby red eyes as if to say, "He's always showing off." She doesn't move. She remains perched, showcasing the beauty that she is.

The remaining twenty plus birds in Ketut's home are tickled every time I pass. I'm not sure why at first, but soon realize that they are so happy that they just let it out to share with every passing stranger.

Ketut gives a giggling smile to the few of us women who wait for our number to be called, and then resends indoors for some lunch. He's only just finished with number 11 and my stomach is starting to rumble. Luckily, Ketut's wife is expecting this.

She lays tiny bananas and other unknown fruits out on the table in her open-air kitchen. She has a small fridge of water and juices. This meal is perfect. It keeps me feeling light as a feather on this day that I'm looking for healing of love sickness. However, I don't feel the love sickness here. There is no longing or worry. In this moment, I can't even recall what I thought I lost.

I take an hour in one of his gardens, the same one with the laughing birds to take pictures of these weasels that I've never seen before. He has pet weasels, or meerkats, or something like that. They are cute. They don't talk and they also don't beg, just like the birds.

I take time to walk and time to sit. But they feel like the same act. I am so happy that I can only feel love and act in gratitude. I pause at every prayer basket and every smiling statue to feel the gratitude. And, every statue is smiling. This is peace.

After several more hours of praying, as this is what I call it now, being still in the moment of gratitude that everything is well, number 18 is called. I decide to define the exact questions that I have for Ketut. I may not get this chance again. It's funny how love changes everything, because at this moment I feel so well that I can't imagine what I'd need to ask of him.

But, when I'm back home, I'm going to wonder, "Where's my man, can I really write a book and how do I get out of my stressful job?"

So, now I'm ready. "Number 19."

I've been participating in his nearly toothless smile all day, but at this moment the essence behind his gentleness is clear. Those lips are giggling. That stomach is itching with laughter. He is one with this home and this place giggles at everything. There is no reason to make life heavy; no reason to make the outside world bigger than the inside world. He's happy to see me approach.

I'm happy, too, but am in shock after flying nearly 20,000 miles for an answer on love to be asked why I don't have a husband.

After five minutes of chatting with me about, well let's call it his intimate life, his mouth goes square and his eyes flat, "Why don't you have a husband?"

I can't believe what I've just been asked. "You tell me!"

He giggles through that peaceful smile and takes the palm of my hand to read it.

"Well, let's see. I see you writing and publishing. You will be rich." A huge mound of laughter erupts. He's so happy for me. "Oh, yes. You will be rich. Don't forget me." He pauses. "Oh, yes. Writing, publishing, you rich. Don't forget me."

I would give up all the money in the world for love. But, he's telling me that being financially rich is my path.

"Once you are rich, you will buy a beauty salon" he continues.

Now this one really throws me.

He is so excited about my life that he just keeps teasing me about what I'll do once I am so rich.

I finally break in. "But what about a love partner?"

"Oh yes," he frowns. "Why don't you keep a man?"

"I haven't found the right man," I retort.

His head hangs a little to the left showing clear disappointment in me.

"Why don't you have a husband?" He is my inquisitor in this subject matter.

I feel a tear in the nape of my eye.

"Don't cry. God gave you everything you need to attract a loving partner. Why do you cry when God gave you these two wrinkles between your eyes to say that you are here to be with a partner? Male and female wrinkles," he says with a huge grin.

I never thought of these two wrinkles this way.

"God gave you good cheekbones and a very good jaw, too. Oh yes, God gave you a good jaw. God gave you smarts and eyes that are off-set just right," he says in a sweet, high-pitched voice. "You have that desire and God gave you what you need. Do not cry when God gives you such things to get your desires filled."

I can't think of anything else to say or ask, because damn it, I have everything I need. Somewhere inside of me, I've known it all along. I feel so complete here and know that he is right, except for maybe the beauty salon. (Well, a beauty salon to him may be one that is to beautify life and uplift the soul. This is real beauty, right?)

I have no questions when I am at peace.

Ketut continues our session by reading the energy lines through my arms, neck and back. He explains that my energy flows well and I should enjoy a long life.

"Enjoy it," he says. "The two big wrinkles on top of your head are from your disappointment in love. I see the pain that you've held in your face. You don't need these. You only need the two wrinkles between your eyes. Male and female wrinkles."

He holds my hands, examines the love lines on my palm, and closes his eyes in silence. When he reopens his eyes, he is serious for my sake but asking me to giggle in life. "I see you had one very short and very painful relationship. But, you have a partner, a boyfriend, who will be with you for the rest of your life. This is a happy partnership." I secretly hope that he is speaking of Paul.

I am so satisfied. I am so complete in the knowing. It's not that he just gave me knowledge; it's that I knew it inside all along but kept my attention from it. My attention is on my inner abundance now, which says that today's prayer worked.

Nyoman, my taxi driver, has an excellent idea that I have dinner at the Crispy Duck in Ubud. It's the perfect open setting, in little bungalows resting atop rice fields, to complete this day sharing duck and rich coffee with so many happy strangers. After the duck, which are quite skinny in Bali, I'm still a little hungry. I order fried bananas topped with vanilla ice cream for both me and Nyoman. Our happiness can be seen by the wrinkles etched by our smiles and felt by the smooth flow of delight down our throats.

The tower of flowers in the lobby of the Conrad makes me feel so welcome. But this doesn't feel half as good as the sound of "Ms. Murphy, Ms. Murphy!" trailing behind me. It's the young man who refused a tip from me last night when he brought my luggage to my room. His smile brightens the night. He's almost out of breath when he catches up to me.

"How was your day Ms. Murphy?" he asks.

"It was fabulous! Bali is so beautiful. I am so happy here."

"Oh yes. Bali is beautiful. Did you get enough rest last night?"

"I rested perfectly last night. Thank you." Of course, I did not.

"Did you eat? Do you need food?"

"I just came from the Crispy Duck. That just might be my favorite restaurant in the world. So, I am not hungry. But, thank you."

"If you get hungry, the restaurants are open. You can call them for room service or I can bring you food on the beach, if you want."

"Thank you so very much, Benito. You are too kind. I'm not hungry right now. I think I'll just go to bed to be ready for tomorrow."

"Very good, Ms. Murphy. Get good rest so you have a good day in Bali tomorrow. Good rest is good for the soul. Namaste," Benito says with his hands cupped in signature prayer.

I bow my head back to honor the divine in him and head to my room for the night.

CHAPTER 20
BALANCE

The teaming brook releases my soul by a symphony. Above the water but beneath a temple, opened by an elephant's mouth, I sit. I try to understand the peace embodied in this hour. I explore what I hear.

The waters play a harmonious melody, a dance of love and laughter with sickness and death. Perfect balance. The beat of drums echoes through my awareness. The water pounds the multitude of earth souls within the rocks. The rocks, in resounding inner strength, say, "hear us and you hear the heart of Mother Earth. Our substance lives, breathes, and dies as all earth beings do, but our spirits remain aware of life and death, so we dance to the flow."

The flow of the waters is the natural flow of life. Gently streaming amidst the rock bed, delighting in the play, and then crashing into the boulder that stops the waters from overflowing into nothingness, the melody is the experience called life. In one moment a violin concerto of light-hearted play is orchestrated. It sounds like the beating of my heart when I am in love. In the next moment, the same concerto turns into a crash and break, merely the ending of that experience so I may grow and become anew. The crash is to keep me aware of this moment. I sit in the center of this play. I can cry or I can dance. Why not dance? The endings are to make better beginnings.

Tears release from my shaded eyes, because my eyes can finally see. I feel the dance. I know the flow. The worry and the questions and the anger and the pain were my unreasonable need to hang on. If I can just be the rocks, observing the flow of life, my mind will be free of worry.

I'm so happy here in this moment that I don't want to leave. I've never experienced true balance until now. I thought balance meant taking life in moderation, not over-eating and not over-doing. This stream of balance is closer to placing awareness in what is happening in the moment and loving it, whether it feels like joy or pain. Balance is allowing the flow of life without getting in the way. Imbalance is being sucked into the human emotions that hold onto everything they know.

My emotions, my sensitivities, are both my weakness and my strength; I choose the strength.

My life is laid out before me in this space half a world away from my home. I was never the rock. I didn't know to love myself enough to take what others did as small. Without self-love as a child, hurtful words and acts from others were the ultimate betrayal. Yet, I didn't know the person they were betraying. That little girl is finally back.

As a young teenager, my pain felt extraordinarily real, the pain of the persona who had taken over the little girl. I wanted to release the pain, so I acted it out. I acted it out as getting attention from boys, creating turmoil with my sister, being sassy with my friends and screaming at my parents. The veil between life and spirit was thin and I longed to get the spirit in me back. But how was I to know that this was the longing? How was I to understand that I am bigger than my emotions and that sensitivities are there to keep me connected? I became smaller while my persona grew larger, and this persona was less able to handle the emotions and in turn, the longing grew. Longing for the Spirit inside, my persona kept pushing farther away from the longing.

I now know where to get energized, healthy and free. Nature. Not Paul. I am turning around.

I feel someone staring at me and finally release the stream and look up to the bridge. Kadek peers through the vines with a concerned gaze.

"Are you well, Rebecca?" Kadek asks.

"Yes, Kadek. I am very happy. Please give me just ten more minutes and you can drive me on to our next stop."

"Of course, Rebecca. Don't rush. I was just worried since you were down by the stream so long and not in the temple."

"I am in the temple, Kadek. Truly, I am in the temple."

"Then this is beautiful to witness, Rebecca. It is this discipline that grows happiness."

He is right. Kadek speaks of another dimension of Creating Forward, as Sara has explained to me, discipline of the subconscious mind. It is the subconscious which creates our circumstances and attracts exactly what it believes. Knowing this balance, staying in the center while joyfully allowing life to flow, helps to remind my subconscious that this is the place of power. Staying in this knowing heals the emotions, making them small and rendering them powerless to attract discord.

Kadek is a person of pure heart and peace. He was my driver for only 15 minutes before he told me that we are friends forever. "You will have many friends in Bali, Rebecca."

My realizations are extensive in this space of perfect balance. I recall the seven stages to grief, which start with denial and proceed through anger and then hit loneliness before hope finally arrives. But, I was stuck in the loneliness stage for far too long. I endured anger, more anger, hate, sorrow, regret, moving on to someone or something else and finally to shear disappointment with a little anger tossed in. If my life's disappointments were clean-cut deaths, I would have had no choice but to proceed through the seven emotional stages. I would have come to accept the reality, gain peace and move on. Instead, my loves told me they wanted to spend their lives with me, and I waited in angst when they denied a commitment to me. I did not experience the first stage of shock because I couldn't believe that they were not with me. Either God would bring them back, because it was 'meant to be' or it was my fault that we separated and I could fix it.

I did not mourn the deaths of my relationships; therefore, I suffered. I awaited their return as if that was the only solution to my happiness. I attached myself to the loss and to the man and yearned for him to return. Even my hate was a yearning. The habitual need to hold the acts that caused my pain kept betrayal as my most real experience in life. If I would have accepted a clean-cut death, I wouldn't have lingered in emotional stagnation. And better yet, if I had only relished the love we shared.

It's good to let things die so the great can be reborn. The circumstances cannot affect what doesn't suffer.

We leave gently and as unnoticed as we arrived. Kadek is not in a hurry. But I am very hungry. I skipped breakfast to make time for writing before Kadek picked me up.

"Do you like shopping?" Kadek asks.

"It depends on what I'm shopping for."

"There is a good market, big market, in Ubud. I take you there, if you like."

"That sounds good. I would like to do that and I'd really like to visit the Monkey Forest in Ubud. Can we go there, Kadek?"

"Yes. It is easy to go there. Every tourist wants to see the Monkey Forest," Kadek responds.

I feel a little dismayed. I don't want to be a regular tourist. "Kadek, I am here for the spirit of the place. I am not a typical tourist. I came here to write a book about spirits and how to find peace. Since Bali is the Island of the Gods, I thought it would be perfect."

"I can take you to many temples."

"I would love that, but can we eat first? I'm really hungry."

"What kind of food would you like?" Kadek asks.

"I want Balinese food, something that I can't get at home."

"I know the perfect place, then. It is close to the Monkey Forest."

Michelle Lucas

I'll try anything so that I can have a different experience. This driving is a different experience. Kadek isn't exactly a slow driver, but he's not in a rush either. It's amazing that a body isn't tossed through the air at this very moment. Around every corner is another being walking into the street, but Kadek just gently glides around them as if they are all in the right place. A mother holding her young, naked son doesn't even notice our presence as the car passes within a meter of her arm. A man crosses in front of us without looking and dogs run everywhere. Yet, Kadek is not surprised and is definitely not disturbed by the jaywalkers.

We come to an abrupt halt. This two-lane road has been made into five lanes by mopeds using both brims and taxis squeezing down the center of the lanes, as if the lines themselves were a lane. About twelve hanged chickens cross my face as I stare in amazement through the window. The moped is carrying another fifty pounds of food around the upside-down chickens. The bags of fruits and vegetables, which could feed a small army, is not the most important item on this moped stand. It is the coconut leaves. The long coconut leaves lie loose in a basket the width of a car, but resting to the driver's back. It is these leaves that are necessary in every practice of the day. One cannot eat or breathe or drive or sing without prayer. It is God who keeps us alive and it is these coconut leaves that the Balinese use repeatedly throughout the day to weave their prayer baskets.

Out the front window I see a woman in the center of a traffic circle raising her prayer basket to the heavens.

The traffic finally breaks but not without a team of mopeds swarming our car, cutting into our path to the restaurant where I must get food. Kadek is still humming and smiling while he glides the car around each intrusive, rude stranger.

"Doesn't that make you angry, Kadek?" I ask.

"Does what make me angry?"

"These people cutting in front of you and walking out into the road? They could get hit and killed."

190

Kadek offers a big smile into the rear-view mirror. "No, Rebecca. They do not make me angry. That would make bad karma for my family."

"Wow. People cutting in front of me make me angry. People who do crazy things on the road make me even madder. They make accidents happen," I explain.

"We just get out of the way, Rebecca. Why does it make you so angry?"

"If I'm trying to get to work and they create an accident, then they make me late for work. When I'm late for work, I get really tense."

Kadek laughs with glee, peering at me inquisitively in the rear-view mirror. "We each have our own place in life Rebecca. It does not help to get angry."

"I know you are probably right, but when I'm late for a deadline, I have so much stress," I say.

"What is a deadline?" Kadek responds.

"It's the end of an event. It is the time in which something has to be completed. If things don't get done by the deadline, then there are bad consequences."

"It sounds like you are chasing death, Rebecca. We don't hurry to the dead line."

I realize that I constantly have a deadline, most of which I place on myself.

"The bad consequences are the karma that our families have if we don't allow everyone their own place in life. Bad karma happens if we choose bad thoughts."

"But, don't you get angry when someone hurts your feelings? What do you do when someone lies to you or betrays you?" Kadek is the fourth Balinese in which I've posed this question.

Now his laugh is a gentle roar. He obviously can't imagine being angry at betrayal, just like the other three. "I can't imagine and I don't want to imagine the karma that would come from being angry at someone when they are the ones not in line with God. There is no reason to be angry at them, but there is a reason to help them."

"Help them?" I ask. "What would you say to someone who betrayed you?"

"I would tell them that their actions are not in balance with the universe or with God. But, there would be no other reaction." Kadek answered like all the others.

I must stop participating in the circus that has become my life. I must walk away from deadlines.

Walking from the car to the restaurant perched to overlook the streets of Ubud, Kadek waves at me as he gets back into the car.

"Aren't you hungry, Kadek? I want to buy you lunch and enjoy conversation with my new friend."

"I ate this morning and I can eat again tonight. My family's festival is tonight and there will be plenty of food. Enjoy Babi Guling," Kadek says.

"I'd love to hear about your family's festival. Will you let me buy you lunch?"

Kadek reluctantly bends to my will, but I can't tell why. I don't know if he wants to spend time away from me or if he believes he is just my driver who shouldn't ask for lunch.

We are escorted upstairs to an open view of rice fields, palms, 20-foot plants bearing majestic crimson flowers and Ubud itself. Two baby pigs with charred heads are pictured on my menu. My stomach jumps. I don't care much for pork, and especially not for the murdering of baby pigs. I wonder if I'll be able to get the food into my mouth.

I order exactly what Kadek orders and it arrives as thin slices of white meat, covered in juicy spices, atop a lump of white rice. Charred bits of what Kadek says are flesh and other parts decorate the rims of the dish. I can't dig in immediately, so I start the conversation that I've been waiting for.

"Kadek, you seem to live in such simple happiness. I really want to understand how you live and know about your family's festival."

"Our families have many festivals Rebecca," Kadek responds.

"We don't have many family festivals at home. We might have one family reunion a year, but these reunions are not a priority. I think this makes Americans a less happy group of people Kadek."

"Without the festival there is no honor of the soul's purpose in life," Kadek purposefully says. He looks down at my food and realizes that I'm only eating the rice. "You should honor the food God has given you Rebecca. My father says to eat in prayer what God gives you and do not leave anything behind. This is disrespectful to the life that was just taken."

His last comment gives me the guilt that I need to taste the meat. It is fabulous, light in texture and delicate in spice.

"Don't eat from guilt Rebecca. Eat with respect, in prayer for all life."

"I miss the celebrations of the inner life, Kadek. This is why I came to Bali. I like visiting the fabulous temples and sites of Bali, but I am not here to visit. I am here to become like the spirit of this place. My home life does not mirror Bali."

This perks Kadek's attention on me more than it has been all day. His raspberry smile perfectly complements his circular face which is now glowing as he watches me dig into my food.

"I am on a spiritual journey in this lifetime, Kadek. I'm writing a book on how to become one with God. But, it's difficult because I have two children who need me, bills to pay, a home to take care of and many other responsibilities. I work at a place where people have warring minds. This does not make me happy. I have to choose between working for money, which is not a reward to me, and living a path that makes me very happy, which is writing books and helping others. I will leave my job soon, but it is difficult because I want to give my children the best. If I lose money, my kids could suffer. I want to give them the best education and the best support in life that I am capable of."

"You have the same journey as my father Rebecca. He struggled also when he had to leave his job for his real work. My brothers and sisters had to take on more work to support the family, but without my father's real work, there is no balance in the family." Kadek says.

"What is your father's real work?"

"He is the leader of family festivals. He used to have a job that paid for our food and other needs, but he started getting very sick. After his sickness returned several times, he knew that it was the dark spirits reminding him that he's really the leader of family festivals and that he must quit his job. Since he quit his job the bad spirits left him alone and his illness has never returned."

"That's exactly what happens to me Kadek. I used to be a biologist but I kept getting sick. The illnesses and accidents wouldn't stop. That is when I knew that I had to leave my job and do my spiritual work. And that was when I was in my early 20's. Now I'm in my forties, with children, and I'm in that same place again. I stopped being happy and I've had several painful surgeries and illnesses since returning to a corporate job. My path is a spiritual path. Speaking from the soul is my true work and I am now returning, but I can't help fearing a difficult consequence for my children. I want to pay for my children's college and if I quit my job, this won't happen. This is why it is more important for me to understand you than to be a visitor of Bali."

"Oh, wow Rebecca! You are like my father. I want you to meet my father. He is a great medicine man. There are many in Bali, but you would like my father because you have the same path in this lifetime."

"Did he adjust easily when he left his job Kadek?"

"It was not easy at first. He felt bad about not providing for us. But we are happier with him leading the festivals. Our family is very healthy because of what he does. It is hard work for him. He coordinates all of the prayers and rituals, food and offerings for every celebration. Our family is very grateful to him. We can celebrate life and build good karma because of his work. He is much healthier and you will be also healthier when you do your real work."

The tug-of-war that is going on inside of me is brutally apparent listening to Kadek. I don't have anyone to pay the bills if I quit my job for my real work, the work that makes me happy to the core. Most days I just struggle to hold my life, home and kids together. I am at work more than I am with my kids. When I'm with my kids, I'm exhausted from work. Without the work there is no home. Without the home, there are no bills. But, I clearly remember that when I did my soul's work before, the bills were always paid. I was provided for repeatedly by surprising sources. I felt it was God that abundance comes from, not the corporate world. If I can live in that knowing again, I will be provided for.

"When you do your soul's work Rebecca the good spirits assist you and you are happy. With happiness comes good health and the energy creates abundance because abundance is the essence that you move into. You must do your soul's work. My father is too busy with our festivals this week for a visit, but when you come back to Bali, you must meet my father," Kadek says.

I realize the glow on Kadek's face is the reflection of his soul's knowing, not the outside world. *My outer world was a reflection of my inner turmoil.*

After a baby monkey tries to steal my camera, I am very glad that I took Kadek's advice not to bring bananas into this forest.

"They will steal your goods so they can trade you for a banana if they know you have one."

After shopping and elephant rides, Kadek takes me back to the hotel where I have much to ponder after this day of wonder. But, I will wonder by participating in this society, one that has taught me the art of balance. For me, participating is engaging in another deep conversation with Hangarsi, now my favorite bartender.

"How was your day Ms. Murphy?" Hangarsi asks.

"Beautiful and eye opening. Being here makes me want to quit my job and focus only on writing books and spiritual work. How are you so happy, Hangarsi?"

"Because I live in Bali," he beams.

"I wish I could live in Bali, but I want to be with my children. I wish I could just go home and quit my job, but I want my children's needs to be met. I love spiritual work and writing, but I can't do it full time because I'd feel like I would be sacrificing my children. Mothers would sacrifice anything for their children, even their own happiness."

"Ms. Murphy, don't sacrifice you. It will not help your children. Do what is in your heart because that is what God wants you to do. God only has your best interest at heart," Hangarsi says.

As I walk the lit paths lined in green foliage and hear the gentle waters of the Bali Sea glide onto the beach, I wonder how I can keep such peace inside of me when I get home. I am not lonely here; yet, the pit of my stomach still feels like a hard lump of clay.

I sit on my balcony in silence but the knot of clay in my gut doesn't dissipate. I want to remove it to heal it; otherwise, I will not find the peace in my heart that is needed to make a decision about my direction in life. I will continue to make bad choices by reacting to pain.

I think of Hangarsi, Kadek and Benito and how they seem to glide through life, as if floating on a gentle river. I think of their smiles and kindness and confidence in life to realize the stark polarity of my fears, regrets, and fear of regret. *They don't have elephants on their backs as I do. In fact, they carry nothing negative on their backs. I'm carrying deadlines on my back.* Kadek's last words to me tonight were to forgive myself and my past so that I may have better dreams. My sleep and dreams have been broken for years. *I should have thanked him more for the excellent advice.*

Now I realize one thing I need to heal any wound left. Forgiveness. I'm not sure who is more difficult to forgive, Paul, my mother or myself. But, it is Paul who sits in the forefront of my mind, so it is Paul who I decide to forgive first, if for anything but to sleep tonight.

I close my eyes as I sit on the lounge chair by the window and try to visualize Paul so I may tell him that I forgive him. I can tell that this will be much easier than it would have been months ago when I was steeped in anger. I try to connect to his soul by visualizing him, but I don't want to see him. I don't want to extend kindness. But, I must for my own sake. I call his name and visualize his face but can only get a few glimpses of a man that I sometimes hate. *This is harder than I thought it would be.*

As I relax more and give up the hate to be in the present moment, I see him. I see Paul. He's naked. I see the reflection of my flat hair in his perfectly bald head. I see one little fat roll just beneath his chest, just like mine. I see his long legs and skinny calves, and feel a little embarrassed that my legs aren't quite as thin as his. And now I see him. I look into his eyes, his puppy dog eyes, those eyes that are unsure of what to do next, reflecting a soul wanting to be born through a mind that does not feel completely safe with its decisions. *He's me! I've been trying to love me!* I fall onto the floor laughing, roaring with a storm of realizations coming into me. I break out into tears with an inability to control the laughter. My ego steps aside. The hate melts. *I can forgive this man!*

CHAPTER 21
Gifts

I know today will be one of splendor. I have forgiven. Forgiving is the one act that releases angst into God's hands. It allows Divine Order. Directing love to the discord consumes that which doesn't belong in God's kingdom. It allowed me to sleep in peace and dream of doves flying higher than eagles. The doves aligned in their intention to love. In flight, they rode the crest of a luminescent wave, soaring above the eagle who was singularly seeking satisfaction from the earth. The doves reached upward, but the eagle was transfixed by the entrails below, being the king of a realm between angels and man.

I awake understanding that hanging onto my vulnerability held me down and turning Paul's behavior over and over in my mind heightened the discord. Only he can forgive his own lies. I can forgive the discord I created from acknowledging them. I now stop the hate in my life, the hate for my circumstances. If Paul did right or wrong is of no consequence to me.

And so is the reason Sara paid no attention to Paul in the field of violets. They stood apart because Sara focuses only on her inner-being. She is not affected by the outer world. I now choose peace within, wherever I am at in the moment.

I slept with the balcony doors wide open to the gathering Monsoon rains and awoke several times. I assumed it was due to the wind, the bats breaking against the mist or the ornery lizard peeking into my room. I now know it was at least all three. Stretching from my bed, the mahogany curtains are battered by the warm wind in a joyful release and the sun is now set to rise unseen. The wedding veils, from behind the curtains, dance in the breeze, stretch toward my bed and bring salt to rest on my lips. The soul of the earth can awaken us all. This day will begin whether I partake in its splendor or not.

I decide that today is a glorious day and I should not waste one moment. Instant and deep-dark coffee beckons and after two cups I decide to pray. I can no longer afford to carry the weight of the elephant on my back. I cannot waste one day in memory of a love lost. I must spend the day in love, even sending that love to Paul. I make prayer the jumping off point for my day.

I tenderly take the prayer basket made of coconut leaves from the night stand and smile in remembrance of Benito's loving smile as he offered it to me yesterday. The winds pick up and the fabrics bring sand and rains to my face. I charge the balcony to retrieve the wind's gifts of palm and wood. The source is too powerful to close the doors. The energy is vacant of thought yet primed to wash through this space. It's not pushing, we are pulling.

Sand and branches and coconut leaves placed neatly in the corner hide the violet petals that were growing just moments ago. First the air is wet but I am dry and then I am drenched in a meltdown of vibrant ecstasy. I want this cleansing; I've been aching for it. My gown sticks to my back and clings to my flesh down to my knees. The trees behind me bend to near breaking, their leaves nearly scraping the sands. A Renoir is painted outside this balcony. What was yesterday greens is today under a spell of gray, stroking the sky for its pleasure. This is my first monsoon, and what a strong one it is.

I quickly place a torn-away coconut leaf in the bottom of the basket. I say I am protected as the tree is by its roots. I am connected to Source and what falls from me was only a once expression no longer needed. What I seemingly lose is only a temporary attachment. I set fire to the rain that once made me feel I needed the fiery expression forever. I find the sun-drenched golden flower that I picked from the path last night and gently place it in the center of my basket. I smile knowing that I can wear this flower in my hair as a symbol that I am single, even though in my forties. I am still youthful. I jump to my feet and scream in exhilaration into the force feeding this coast. No one could possibly hear me above the shatters. I scream from my soul that I am forever youthful and not attached to the thoughts of age. I am single and youthful and spirited to live a fresh experience every day of my life.

Across this island, wind kicks these flowers, these rays of sun, from their stems, as if the created beauty is not supposed to cling to its source. She will soon wither, but not before I recognize her delicate beauty and how grateful I am to live amongst this beauty on Earth. I proceed in the prayer by thanking God for flowers and for the abundance in which we live. I don't plead to God or ask for what I don't have. God doesn't sit back and watch us suffer, just waiting for us to plead for help.

I want to add the juniper beads that I received from a Navajo friend in Colorado, so I reach into my purse to retrieve them. But my hand does not behold the beads when I open it. Lying in my palm is assorted nuts from the airplane, and in the center, in the center of my palm is that wheat penny I found perched on my window pane over a year ago. That wheat penny could have only been gifted from my grandfather who passed away over a decade ago. He was an avid collector of these wheat pennies and he has never left my side.

I add banana skins and a few sprinkles of rice to the basket and relax into the essence of my own life, my heart. It expands as I focus on God, the Good.

The basket jumps with joy in the rhythm of the waves crashing to shore outside. My eyes are sprinkled by the mist, forcing my eyelids shut. They stick together for a moment when I too feel this rush of joy within. An elephant appears before me saying that I am now strong enough to recognize the turmoil around me without giving it a thought. With the next rush of salt water waves, a large sea turtle swims near and I feel her strength through gentleness. She rides the waves with ease and without taking on the emotional waters. I will now practice her approach. The warm air dives, scooping up a great-horned owl, bringing him to rest on my left shoulder. He peers only ahead not looking at me as he addresses the need to see through the darkness, always. He promises to remain with me and assist in keeping my sight on the light under all circumstances.

My sticky eyelashes don't want to open, but I make them. My emotions want to remember the pain, but I don't let them. This is another dimension of creating forward, to take authority. I command my heart to take front and center of my life and to guide me. I command my love to ignore the worries, feelings of separation and other basic instincts.

I can now focus on the love of my heart and know that love has been flowing to me, even through Paul. I have released the thoughts untrue to the heart, those of discord, and allow my heart to receive the blessings that are everywhere. I know the heart only expands love. I finally understand Sara's instructions to not withdraw love and to perceive everything from the point of love.

Holding the basket, I pray from my heart, knowing that we are all one and all love. I intend to expand this consciousness into my life. It is my consciousness, not the prayer basket that creates miracles. My consciousness from the point of love is the activity that will create my new life. I see my gifts, my joy, my writing and all of my expressions as that which I am to expand. These are my gifts that I am here to expand.

The monsoons return to their source this mid-afternoon Bali day and how glorious the last several hours have been. Resting with my now book, as I can no longer call it my journal, within an enclosed canopy I've been writing to rains battering the windows for hours. I now await a chance to hail a taxi for my next gift.

"Capa Louac" my driver pleads. "You must have some."

I'm curious why the five coffees that I just drank were free and this one will be about twice the amount of a cup of Starbucks. The coffees are so rich and this last one the richest. They want me to purchase some to take home, but it is so very expensive. I just take in this amazing landscape of layered rice fields, one on top of the other, the coffee bean trees, the two extremely large bats hanging upside down at the entrance and those cats, the same cats that were at Ketut's home. Everyone just laughs with wide eyes waiting for my response. "Do you like the coffee Louac Ms. Murphy?"

I'm really enjoying this night air and the kindness of Hangsari. He gifts me with an extra shot of vodka which reminds me of the extra shot of coffee.

"I drank a coffee today that was really expensive. Everything is so cheap here that I was surprised. Why is coffee Louac so expensive? What is special about it?"

His eyes are as wide and twinkling as the men who offered the coffee. "Rebecca, it is because of what the farmers have to do to make that coffee. It's dirty work."

"What do you mean?"

He laughs such a delightful laugh, but I can tell he knows a secret that I do not.

"The louac eats the beans and then you know what happens? The farmers pick out the beans to make them into coffee. Do you know what I mean Ms. Murphy?

"No" I honestly respond.

"The farmers pick out the digested beans."

Oh damn.

"You are such a gift," I tell Hangsari.

"And Rebecca, those farmers gave you a gift today. You can now say you had Coffee Louac."

CHAPTER 22
Plotless

He awakens me mid-dream, in the midst of a song to one day etch in my mind for the strands of time. A choir sang of inner peace. A peace that I now understand to be paramount to the health of my body.

I am rested and aware that it is early morning. Harry the Gila Monster breaks leaves outside my open window, rattling me from my sleep, as he typically does. I breathe in this new day, excited to get to my writing. While awakening, I know that I'm in my bed and it is still dark outside. The Head of Charity peers down at me from the wall above as She always does. *Ah, Raphael.*

Stillness outside, except for Harry and a parade of the desert pheasants walking their young through my manzanita and of course, the gentle, cool breeze.

My favorite book lies open on my nightstand. *On Writing*, by Stephen King. I smile in remembrance of his advice, to disregard a plot for your novel. Advice that I have come to take personally. I lay for a moment in the sweet gratitude that it is the first day of spring, I am in my 52nd year and I found happiness by disregarding a plot for my life.

As Stephen King explained, with a plot, the character does not get to unfold because the character is stuck inside boundaries. Instead of focusing on a way to get through my boundaries and asking "why, why why is this happening?", I have allowed my gifts to pull me forward. And the pulling now feels like a standing ovation!

It's been forty-five years since I sat rocking with my grandparents on their front porch. We had finished painting the prior day, a painting job that has yet to be erased. Grandpa had given me a paint brush to help him paint the exterior of his house. I was still quite short and definitely was not going to be climbing any ladders. The paint brush was small, so what harm could I do? Dipping the brush into the green paint and slapping it onto the canvas of my grandpa's house was fun. I dipped it over and over again, watching the paint mound more and more on the bristles. The more paint that I put on the house the more excited I became. I can't remember how I dislodged the drop cloth beneath me. I was probably acting, since every move had a drama written within. I probably did a twirl, but it really doesn't matter. What matters is that when my grandpa was high on the ladder, the drop cloth went highly missing from the porch. I let my paint brush take a big dip into the pail of green. I wanted to slap it onto a piece of white but the paint did not make it that far. A big dollop landed smack on the porch concrete floor. Oops. I tried to wipe it up. I ran to get water. Water did nothing. I pulled over the heavy drop cloth and wiped and wiped that dollop of green paint over and over again. The green just grew larger on the floor. I don't know how I came up with this idea and it doesn't matter. My idea became etched into the porch for eternity. I thought I'd just make the entire porch green. So I painted and painted and painted some more, to hopefully be done before my grandpa got off of that ladder. But when I reached the seven stairs that led down to the street, I realized that a green porch with grayish stairs looked silly. So, I kept painting, all the way down to the street. The oldest house in my old home town is still garnished with green. Emerald Green. My grandparents were not mad, as they never were. So, we just rocked on that porch while drinking some peppermint tea the following day. Their minister came to minister to them, as they had lost 3 children in their lives and could definitely use all of the compassion that could be given. Yet, I witnessed something else. My grandparents just listened to the minister as he talked and talked. They were the ones with the open hearts. He was there to receive their love, although unintentionally. Love is in the silence.

It's been twenty years since angels held onto my body as I popped through my belly and travelled beyond time. I believed that experience would lock me into the good life forever, since I returned with a love beyond the human realm. But it did not. I communicated this experience with everyone that I could, so they would hold hope in their hearts for a loving life realized. I was not silent. My thoughts were still not calm because I focused on the pain of others and wanted to fix their problems. I did not want them to hurt. I learned and I mean, I learned a lot! Focusing on a problem is a problem and it is control and it is interference. This did not happen on that beautiful sphere of light at the end of my out-of-body journey. In silence, those beings, an existence in which humanity is moving toward, act from an inner light that restores all to a healthy condition.

It's been ten years since I had the peculiar thought of dedicating a book to myself, in an act of self-love in the midst of despair. My story looked bleak. I saw no way out of my pain. Shingles in my left eyeball cuffed me to the couch with nowhere to go and nothing to do but feel the pain. That's when I grabbed my journals. Reading all of my words from the past with my right eye, an idea started to arise in me that I could write myself out of despair. It would be years later that I realized how I was using a gift to free myself. It would be years later that I came face to face with my gifts through the words of Ketut Leyer, Kadek and many other grateful people of Bali. I came to realize that each individual has a unique gift and that gift is there to pull them forward. *If they would just take the time to find it.* It would be years before I fully accepted my path, as Kadek's father did. I had several more illnesses and injuries before taking the hint. Those illnesses and injuries were completely unnecessary.

It's been seven years since I jumped off my destitute train. While driving to work, I realized that I was wearing white skinny pants, a blue-ruffled shirt and high heels. Amethysts, jaspers, fluorites and hematite wrapped around my wrists. My favorite rose quartz hung from my neck. I wondered why I had not worn the khakis and polo shirt that was the appropriate attire for my job. I had laid the clothes out on my bed the night before. From deep inside, something was taking over my actions. In my car, on the way to work, I realized that this would be a very different day. As the morning rolled on, I observed myself removing my personal items from my desk. First a coffee mug, then a couple of books and finally all of the hair ties that I had collected in the deep recesses of that dark desk. One by one, I walked each item to my car. I hadn't seen Paul in nearly two years and when I walked back from my car, after leaving it with my last personal item, he was standing at my desk. Paul. A feeling so deep welled up inside of me that I couldn't resist its energy. Love. In that moment, the love for Paul did not matter. The love for myself mattered. I walked out to my car, drove home and never returned.

I was a little shocked with my new circumstances. No paycheck. No ability to pay for my children's college expenses. And then it came. A letter in the mail. Only two weeks after jumping off the train, Marisha received a full-ride scholarship. Oh yes, she had been offered several partial scholarships to colleges in the South, colleges closer to her family and friends. But this one scholarship was big! Colorado State University.

It's been six years since I've seen the swamps and the Cane River, that starting place of my novel.

It's been five years since I stopped using the term 'God' since the word denotes that something separate from us decides to give us pain or give us peace. I saw the Oneness. I saw how every consciousness determines the whole. Therefore, I place gratitude into the Oneness so that goodness is manifest. I focus on gratitude so that everything that one could be grateful for may be seen on Earth.

It's been four years since I laid on my healing table in the room of my brand new mountain-view home and forgave my mother, in my heart and soul. Days later I finally returned to the best darn massage therapist around, Nikki. The door wasn't even shut behind me when she said, "Your face has changed. You've done forgiveness work and you look so much better, it shows in your face!" And it's been four years since all of my pain vanished.

Our inner condition determines our outer condition. I thought of my gift, these two wrinkles between my eyes. Male and female wrinkles. I thought of Albert's advice, that love is all that matters. I called Paul. I told him that I loved him and that I wish him only peace. I stayed with only positive triggers in my mind. Like Sara, when we think of beauty, we are beauty. I developed a positive trigger. Molasses. Sweet Molasses. *Thank you grandpa.* May my life bring with it all that is sweet to everyone my life may touch.

It's been one year since I awoke to the understanding that I have gained the inner substance I was looking for. It's been a process and a process well worth living. The well-lived life has no plot. I no longer solve problems in the linear way, as it is the linear mind that creates the problems. I re-read my memoir and released the struggle. I use my gifts as my beacon of Light.

It's been 6 months since my memoir became a novel. I smile and stretch my arms toward the ceiling as the lion's sun sends a golden ray of light through my window to reach me, as if to reach only me.

Paul's gentle lips kiss my cheek and his fingers caress my back. "Good morning my love. Your phone has been ringing a few times already this morning. I did not want to wake you," he whispers in my ear.

"Good morning Paul." I turn and wrap my arms around him and lay my freshly kissed cheek upon his bare chest before checking my phone.

I return the call to one of my newest acquaintances, Concetta, and she does not say hello, but starts the conversation with "You just sold a million copies!"

Namaste,
Rebecca Hope Murphy

P.S. After the first run at my book and shortly after I refused to loan *On Writing* out to anyone, Sara returned in my dreams. My hair was much shorter and back to its natural brown. I saw it in the mirror by which she stood. She had a big smile on her face, even though I was looking out the door in hopes that I'd see Paul.

She handed me a piece of paper and said "Michelle, give them this book." In big bold letters strewn across the face of a piece of parchment it read: ***Why Elephants Never Lie***

Acknowledgements

Grandpa & Grandma: Thank you for your love, the cabbage and potatoes, the sweet molasses, your presence each time I wrote, and for giving birth to my mother.

My son, Dakota: Thank you for your love, your patience, your understanding and for being my son. May all of the blessings that you have given me be given back to you in spades.

My daughter, Cheyenne: Thank you for your love, your patience, your understanding and for being my daughter. May all of the blessings that you have given me be given back to you in spades.

Greg: Thank you for your presence, your understanding and your patience. The next book will be dedicated to your sister. May all of the blessings that you have given me be given back to you in spades.

My best friend, Albert: Thank you for your love and your presence. Thank you for writing *Irene*, at a time when I needed it the most.

Tina Harrington: Thank you for the "kick in the butt."

Jovita and Mable "Legs" McCloud: Thank you for the job when I needed it the most and thank you to Sedona Crystal Vortex.

Virginia, Rachel, Jo, Cheyenne, Sassy, Pigtail Pearl, Clementine, Petunia, Scratchy, Andi, Dixie, Dr. Quinn, K, M & Concetta: Thank you for ending the story with me. It's been fun!

CREATINGFORWARD.COM, My heart-felt gratitude to Duane, Samantha, Renee and Julie

Made in the USA
San Bernardino, CA
29 June 2020

74627563R00139